FOUNDED 1869 *Patron* HER MAJESTY THE QUEEN

The Teaching of Swimming

14th Revised Edition 1987
ISBN 0 900052 17.1

PUBLISHED BY
THE AMATEUR SWIMMING ASSOCIATION
IN LIAISON WITH THE SWIMMING TIMES LTD.

AMATEUR SWIMMING ASSOCIATION
TEACHERS CERTIFICATES FOR SWIMMING

Current syllabuses and further details from:
Harold Fern House
Derby Square, Loughborough, Leicestershire LE11 0AL

ISBN 0 900052 17.1

Printed by Leicester Printers Ltd. 99 Church Gate, Leicester

Contents

Preface

This is the fourteenth edition of *The Teaching of Swimming* and like those which it follows, it derives from the extensive practical experience of swimmers, teachers and coaches throughout the country.

The previous editions have been widely read and it is the earnest wish of the Education Committee that this one will continue to provide sound advice and guidance for those seeking to improve their knowledge of swimming and their effectiveness as teachers.

An attempt has been made to give a comprehensive yet concise cover of all aspects related to the teaching of swimming. However, emphasis has been placed on the more practical aspects, with theoretical considerations kept to the relevant minimum.

The practices described are by no means exhaustive, nor is it suggested that these should be followed exclusively. It should be said, however, that all of them have been used to good effect and found successful.

The format has been retained for it is felt that it does present the material in a manner that facilitates reference to the more significant factors and essential features.

This new edition reiterates all contained in previous editions, and, keeping abreast with current development, there is an addition to the section dealing with resuscitation.

A. H. Cregeen
Honorary Editor

Produced on behalf of the Amateur Swimming Association by:–
Messrs A. H. Cregeen, A. Donlan, J. M. Noble, T. G. Thomas (Education Committee – Publications), J. Verrier (Co-opted), B. E. Gorton (NDO), with the assistance of Mrs J. Gray (NDO).
The ASA acknowledges the assistance of the RLSS and of Dr Anthony Handley, MD, FRCP, Medical Adviser to the RLSS.

Introduction

Although water is not their natural habitat, nevertheless most people are endowed with physical attributes which allow them to float in it. Once this phenomenon is experienced, appropriate actions of the limbs will bring about the movement known as swimming. This exhilarating activity is for all, from the very young to the very old, from the frail to the strong, from the physically handicapped to the athletic.

Throughout this country there is ample provision for people to swim and there are many very good reasons why everyone should learn to do so, as the following aims will indicate.

Survival

There is an ever present danger in the extent of open water to be found in this country, in sea, rivers, lakes, canals and disused pits. Every year a large number of deaths are caused through drowning, many of these occurring within a few metres of safety. It is very important, therefore, that all should be able to swim, not only to save themselves in an emergency, but also to avoid the needless endangering of the lives of rescuers. This same open water provides opportunities for a wide range of activities such as sailing, surfing, canoeing and ski-ing, for which swimming is a prerequisite.

Recreation

In these days of increased leisure time, the need for involvement in some kind of recreational pursuit, preferably of a physical nature, is generally recognised. Swimming provides the means and it has many advantages:

a) Ample opportunities are available in swimming pools and leisure centres; also in open water, providing there is adequate supervision and suitable weather.
b) Little equipment is required, simply a costume and towel.
c) It is comparatively inexpensive.
d) It can be enjoyed in company or alone, but there should be supervision.
e) Age is no barrier. Babes together with parents enjoy movement in water and old people can continue to swim when other recreative pursuits might prove too strenuous.
f) It allows for family participation, including any member who might be disabled.
g) Membership of swimming clubs provides social opportunities as well as facilities for training and the development of swimming skills.

Therapy

Swimming can be valuable in medical treatment and in general therapy for the following reasons:
a) The supportive nature of water permits the performance of gentle movement without undue tension, thereby assisting in rehabilitation after injury or illness.
b) The disabled and physically handicapped may take part because weight bearing is not required. Movement and travel can take place without the use of great strength and the performer is able to experience and enjoy a freedom of movement not possible out of water.

c) It is particularly suited to the overweight person whose obesity is not so noticeable in water. The condition itself assists flotation and hence, the ability to swim. Through exercise, heart and blood vessels can be strengthened and in swimming, muscles can be worked and joints taken beyond their normal range. Similar movements attempted on land would be stressful.
d) For all people, swimming is an enjoyable way of keeping fit. It improves stamina and stimulates the circulatory and respiratory systems, thereby promoting a feeling of general well-being.

Competition

Most people swim for reasons already stated. Some may wish to improve their skill by means of self imposed challenges, or by preparing for various tests. Many of these are promoted by the Amateur Swimming Association. For those endowed with special abilities and aptitudes there are many opportunities for participation in swimming as a competitive sport. For such people, coaching, training and swimming events are provided by the many clubs to be found throughout the country.

Chapter 1

The Scientific Principles of Swimming

A comprehensive study of the scientific principles involves a knowledge and understanding of mechanics, hydrostatics, fluid mechanics and, of course, the anatomy and physiology of the human body.

Flotation and Density

The ability of an object to float depends upon the density of the substance from which it is made and the density of the liquid in which it is placed. Most discussions on flotation are concerned with objects which float in water but it is important to remember that solids which will not float in water will float in other liquids. For example, a solid lump of lead will not float in water but it will float in mercury. However, a thin sheet of lead formed into a watertight box can be made to float in water, depending upon the changed density.

The density of any substance or object is found by dividing its mass (grams) by its volume (cubic centimetres).

Therefore density = mass ÷ volume
= grams ÷ ccs

(Sometimes the term 'weight' is used in place of 'mass' but the correct term is 'mass').

Some examples of substances and their densities are given in the table. Two liquids (water and mercury) are included. All the substances above each liquid will float in it whilst those below will sink.

All the substances with a density less than water will float in it and those with a greater density will sink. Salt has a density of 2.17g per cc so that when it dissolves the density of salt water is greater than fresh water.

Substance	Density g per cc
Air	0.0129
Cork	0.24
Oak	0.65
Fat (human)	0.90
Ice	0.92
Female (human)	0.97
Male (human)	0.98
Water	1.00
Bone (human)	1.85
Concrete	2.40
Aluminium	2.70
Iron (wrought)	7.80
Lead	11.30
Mercury	13.50
Gold	19.30
Platinum	21.50

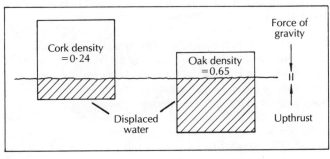

Fig. 1·1

As the density of the solid gets nearer to that of the liquid it will float with more of its volume submerged. Ice with a density of 0.92g/cc floats with 92% of its volume submerged, i.e. only 8% of an iceberg is visible above the water!

The density of a hollow object can be altered by filling or emptying the space. A well-known example of this is the submarine which has ballast tanks which allow it to float at the surface when empty and to sink below it when filled with sea water (fig. 1·2).

In a similar manner, the human body floats higher in the water when the lungs are filled with air. In this case, the volume of the chest increases with little increase in mass.

Upthrust
Any object placed in a liquid is subjected to an upward force (upthrust) from the liquid. When an object is floating on the surface, the upthrust balances the force of gravity acting downwards.

Upthrust = weight of displaced water
Force of gravity = weight of object

Some human beings (good floaters) can float horizontally whilst others can only float vertically with the head above the water (poor floaters). Good floaters have a more even density throughout the body whilst poor floaters have higher density legs and trunk (fig. 1·3).

In general terms, younger children are good floaters but as they get older, their body density changes. Females tend to remain good floaters whilst adult males tend to develop muscular, and therefore, high density bodies. The buoyancy (ability to float) of the body is an important factor in swimming. Muscular swimmers will tend to float lower in the water whilst those with a higher proportion of fatty tissues will be high floaters. Due to their physical structure a small proportion of human beings are unable to float.

Propulsion
The movement of a body through the water depends upon the size of the propulsive force and its direction. During the early stages of swimming, movement through the water is governed very largely by Isaac Newton's Third Law of Motion which states that *for every action (force) in one direction there is an equal and opposite reaction (force) in the opposite direction.*

A simple and easily understood application of this law arises when paddling a canoe. The canoeist pushes the paddle towards the rear of the craft (action) and the canoe moves in the forward direction (reaction) (fig. 1·4).

In swimming, the hands and arms act rather like the paddles of a canoe. The greatest amount of propulsion occurs when the arms are moving backwards (fig. 1·5).

This third law of Newton applies to every aspect of all strokes and consequently a downward action of the limbs produces an upward reaction in the body. For example, the downward movement of the limbs during the Butterfly Stroke causes the body to move in the opposite direction (upward) (figs. 1·6).

Swimmers with very flexible ankle joints can make use of this flexibility by using the feet as flippers and, as a result, gain additional forward movement.

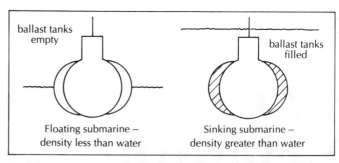

Fig. 1·2

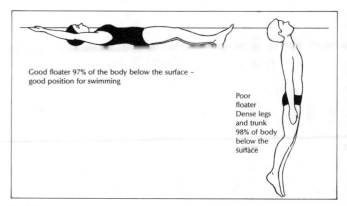

Fig. 1·3

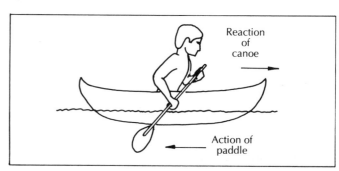

Fig. 1·4

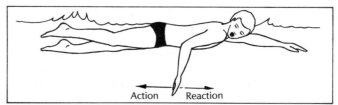

Fig. 1·5

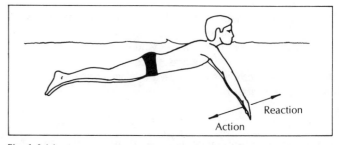

Fig. 1·6 (a)

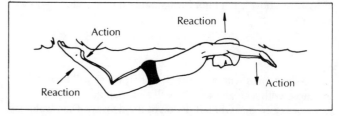

Fig. 1·6 (b)

Highly skilled competitive swimmers do not move their arms directly backward during propulsion because there are other forces which must be taken into consideration. A detailed explanation of these forces is beyond the scope of this book but the basic principles are given below and are based on the factors which permit an aeroplane to lift off the ground. The shape of the wing is such that air travels much faster over the top of the wing than across the underside which results in a high pressure area being created under the wing and a lower pressure above the wing causing the aircraft to be lifted off the ground (figs. 1·7). The same principle applies to the movement of any object through a fluid (which includes air and water). The amount of lift given to the swimmer depends upon;

a) the shape of the cross section of the hand,

b) the speed with which the hand moves relative to the water,

c) the angle which the hand makes with the direction of pull.

Experienced swimmers, constantly striving for a better performance, attempt to position the hand at an angle which gives maximum thrust. In achieving this, the hand is seen to change its pathway as it presses against the water. This is an aspect of fluid mechanics known as Bernoulli's Principle and explains such phenomena as the 'keyhole' pull in the Butterfly Stroke (fig. 1·8).

Body Shape and Streamlining
The ideal body shape for moving through the water (i.e. submerged) is that developed by sea creatures. The sailfish is reputed to have reached speeds in excess of 100km per hour. A world class sprint swimmer partly submerged, reaches speeds of about 7.2km per hour over a distance of 100 metres. For generations, man has studied the factors which determine how efficiently ships move through water and one of the most important of these for speed is streamlining.

For maximum performance, human beings must adopt a position which provides the greatest streamlining of the body, i.e. horizontal with arms stretched beyond the ears and meeting in front of the head thereby offering minimal frontal resistance(figs. 1·9).

The body shape also has some effect. The tall and slim person may have mechanical advantage and better streamlining but less power than the stocky person who must sacrifice some streamlining for muscular bulk.

Resistance to Motion

Frontal resistance
When an object moves through a fluid it meets a resistance. A common example of this occurs when riding a bicycle. A large person will experience a greater total resistance than a small one. The greater the speed, the greater is the air resistance experienced. Thus, frontal resistance depends upon the shape of the object, its speed and the density of the fluid. It can be kept to a minimum by adopting a streamlined shape (figs. 1·9).

An additional source of profile resistance comes from swimwear. When swimming, water moves between the body and the swimwear thus increasing resistance. This emphasises the need for well designed good fitting swimwear for maximum performance.

Eddy current resistance
Eddy currents cause turbulence behind objects moving through fluids and this is greatest where the object has the least

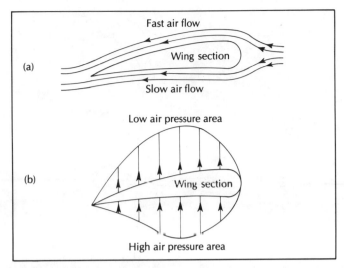

Fig. 1·7

Fig. 1.8

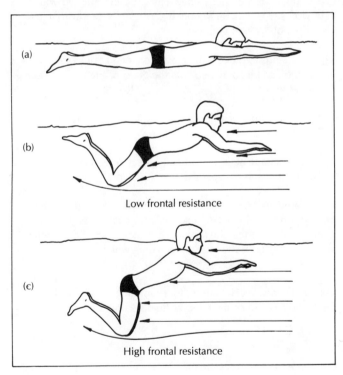

Fig. 1·9

streamlining. The effect of eddy currents is to create a drag which reduces forward motion. In recent years the reduction of eddy current drag has featured high on the priority of motor car designers since its reduction has the effect of producing greater efficiency and consequently a reduction in fuel consumption. It is difficult to alter the shape of a swimmer but better streamlining can be obtained by adjustments to the position of the body in the water (fig. 1·10).

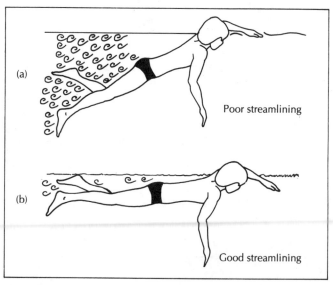

(a) Poor streamlining

(b) Good streamlining

Fig. 1·10

Similarly, in swimming, the formation of eddy currents is wasteful of energy and reduces efficiency.

Eddy currents may be formed in the spaces between hairs and for this reason some swimmers have been known to shave their legs. However, there does not appear to be any scientific measurement of this effect.

Viscous drag

Every liquid has a property known as viscosity. A liquid with a high viscosity is difficult to pour e.g. oil, whilst one with a low viscosity pours easily e.g. water.

Viscosity tends to prevent the movement of an object through a liquid and can be compared with the effect of friction between two solid surfaces.

As the temperature of a liquid falls, the viscosity increases. Thus, cold water has a higher viscosity than warm water.

The viscous force acting against an object moving through a liquid increases as the speed of the object increases.

Considering the effect of viscosity on a swimmer leads to the conclusion that viscous drag is greater in cold water than in warm water, and that the faster a swimmer moves through the water the greater is the total viscous drag which must be overcome.

In recent years, special fabrics for swimming attire have been developed to reduce the effect of fluid friction to a minimum.

It is important to appreciate that these various forms of resistance are inextricably interdependent. For example, improved streamlining reduces the effect of profile resistance and viscous drag. In this chapter each form of resistance has been treated individually, but all forms of resistance are experienced simultaneously.

Reader's notes

Reader's notes

Chapter 2

Anatomy and Physiology

Circulation, Breathing and Respiration

An essential feature of all living mammals including man is the circulation of the blood since it provides the main transport medium in the body. The major functions of blood are;

a)   to transport oxygen from the lungs to the body tissues,

b)   to transport carbon dioxide from body tissues to the lungs,

c)   to transport digested foods to meet the body's requirements,

d)   to transport naturally made poisons (e.g. urea) to the kidneys,

e)   to regulate body temperature.

This chapter is concerned primarily with the first two of these functions and the changes in them which are necessary when the body is subjected to exercise. In order to appreciate fully the processes involved, it is essential to have a clear, if elementary, understanding of blood circulation, the mechanism of breathing, tissue respiration, and how these change to meet the additional requirements of exercise.

Blood Circulation

The main organs of the circulatory system are the heart, lungs and blood vessels. The heart is essentially a pump divided into two entirely separate sections by a muscular wall called the septum. Each of these two major sections has a smaller upper chamber called the atrium (auricle) and a larger lower chamber called the ventricle. Valves allow blood to flow from the atria to the ventricles but not in the reverse direction (fig. 2·1). The blood passes through two systems, the pulmonary circulation which directs blood from the heart to the lungs and back to the heart, while the systemic circulation carries the blood to and from the remaining organs and tissues of the body. The pressure which directs the blood around the body comes from the left ventricle and therefore, the muscular wall making up this chamber is considerably thicker than the rest of the heart muscle. The de-oxygenated blood from the body enters the right atrium through the main veins (inferior and superior vena cavae), passing next through a one-way valve into the right ventricle. From here, the blood is pumped through the pulmonary artery to the lungs where it gives up carbon dioxide in exchange for oxygen. The re-oxygenated blood then returns to the left atrium through the pulmonary vein and passes down through a one-way valve into the left ventricle. The powerful muscular walls of the left ventricle then contract and force out the blood through the aorta and round the body. From the aorta, the blood passes into successively smaller arteries and eventually into the capillaries

(fig. 2·2) which permeate the body tissue. The walls of these capillaries consist of a single layer of body cells which allow water and all dissolved substances, except for the larger protein molecules to pass through. Tissue fluid flows away from the capillaries to the body cells where oxygen is extracted and waste products, particularly carbon dioxide, are absorbed into the blood stream from these body cells. Some of this tissue fluid is re-absorbed by the blood which then flows into the veins and back to the heart.

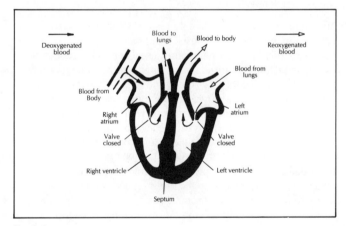

Fig. 2·1

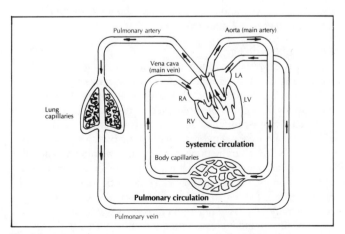

Fig. 2·2

The Mechanism of Breathing

The main organs involved in breathing are the trachea (wind-pipe), the left and right bronchus (one to each lung), bronchioles, air-sacs and alveoli (fig. 2·3). As air enters the nasal passages it is warmed to body temperature, humidified, and filtered by small hairs and mucus. The trachea (wind-pipe) is the main airway from the back of the throat and consists of C-shaped rings of cartilage which prevent the walls from collapsing and thus keep the airway clear. The trachea splits into two bronchi, one to each lung. The small branches of the system called bronchioles, carry the air to ducts which terminate in air-sacs or alveoli. Each alveolus which is about 0.2mm in diameter, has the appearance of a bubble and has a surface covered by a network of capillaries. The structure of a lung follows a similar pattern to that of a large bunch of grapes. The lungs and the heart are contained inside the chest or thorax. The internal surface of the thoracic cavity and the outer surfaces of the lungs are lined by the pleura, a double layer of membrane, containing a fluid which acts as a lubricant, reducing friction where the lungs move in contact with the rib cage during breathing. The expansion and contraction of the lungs which allows air to enter (inhalation) or leave (exhalation) is caused by the muscular movements of the thoracic boundaries. The insides of the lungs are continuously open to the atmosphere whilst the thoracic cavity is completely enclosed. This results in a difference in air pressure between the inside of the lungs and the thoracic cavity so that the pressure in the lungs is always higher. This higher lung pressure has two very important effects;

a) it causes the walls of the alveoli to stretch so that the lungs almost fill the thoracic cavity completely,

b) it ensures that during breathing, when the volume of the thoracic cavity increases, the lungs inflate to fill all the available space completely.

The increase in volume of the thoracic cavity is caused by changes in the intercostal muscles and in a dome-shaped muscle called the diaphragm, which forms a seal across the base of the cavity. Inhalation is caused by the simultaneous contraction of the diaphragm and the inter-costal muscles. When the diaphragm contracts a central region moves down so that the muscle becomes flatter. Simultaneously, the inter-costal muscles between ribs contract which causes the rib cage to rise upwards and outwards thus increasing the volume of the thoracic cavity. This upward and outward movement of the rib cage is only possible because the ribs pivot at the points where they are attached to the spine and to the breast bone (sternum). The increase in volume of the thoracic cavity automatically causes an increase in the lung volume. As the volume of the thoracic cavity increases, air flows into the lungs from the atmosphere to occupy the additional space and stops only when the pressure inside the lungs reaches the same value as the atmosphere outside. When exhalation occurs, the diaphragm and the inter-costal muscles relax causing a decrease in the volume of the thoracic cavity and forcing air out of the lungs to the open atmosphere (figs. 2·4 and 2·5).

Control of Breathing

There is wide variation in the natural breathing rates of individuals which depend on factors such as fitness, general health and the anatomy and physiology of the individual. For most adults the normal breathing rate when relaxed is between 12 to 18 times per minute. During times of exertion, both the volume of air involved in breathing and the breathing rate increase. Although individuals can control breathing rate and the volume of air being moved, there are times when breathing is a reflex action i.e. occurs automatically and is beyond the control of individuals. During an energetic swimming session (or any other activity), the level of carbon dioxide (CO_2) in the blood rises because of the increased production of this gas in the muscle tissues. The nerve-endings in the walls of some arteries

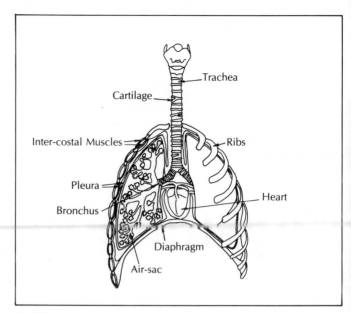

Fig. 2·3

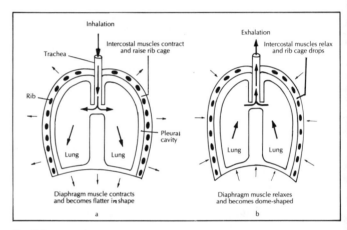

Fig. 2·4

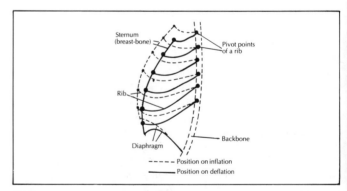

Fig. 2·5

react to this increased carbon dioxide concentration and cause impulses to be sent to the respiratory centres of the brain which result in an automatic increase in the depth and rate of breathing. The total volume of the lungs of an adult human being is about 5 litres. During relaxed breathing, only about ½ litre of air moves in and out of the lungs. This is known as the *tidal* volume. Additional air can be drawn into the lungs at will and this is known as the *complemental* volume of air. Similarly, about 1½ litres of air can be forcibly exhaled and this is known as the *supplemental* volume. After the supplemental volume has been forced out, there remains in the lungs about 1½ litres of air known as the *residual* volume. This occurs because the chest cannot be completely collapsed.

Respiration

Respiration is the name given to the chemical processes that take place in the body cells which enable the body to produce the energy necessary for its vital functioning. The energy of the body is obtained from glucose (a type of sugar manufactured in the body from foodstuffs) plus oxygen. The chemical changes which take place to produce this energy involve more than fifty steps but these may be greatly simplified in the following equation.

$$Glucose + Oxygen \rightarrow Carbon\ Dioxide + Water + Energy$$

The fifty or so intermediate steps occur in two main stages. In the first stage, only a small amount of energy is released and no extra oxygen is required. This is known as anaerobic (without oxygen) respiration. During this stage several intermediate substances are produced one of them being lactic acid. Under conditions of extreme exertion or repeated attempts by an unskilled swimmer, the oxygen supply to the muscles cannot be maintained at a sufficiently high level. This gives rise to the second stage in the chain of reactions where complete breakdown of the intermediate substances occurs. Under these conditions a supply of oxygen is essential. This stage is known as aerobic (with oxygen) respiration.

During conditions of extreme exertion the energy supplied to the muscles comes mainly from anaerobic respiration and lactic acid is produced faster than it can be broken down by the aerobic stage in the chain. As a consequence, there is a build-up of lactic acid in the muscles. If physical exertion continues at a high rate, the time is reached when the amount of lactic acid in the body system prevents further muscular activity until sufficient oxygen is absorbed via the lungs to counteract the acid. However, it is possible for muscles to continue working for sometime with an inadequate oxygen supply, when the body can be said to be incurring an oxygen debt. It is for this reason that heavy breathing continues for sometime after strenuous exercise. This rapid breathing phase is referred to by swimmers and other athletes as the recovery period.

The Principal Adaptations of the Body to Exercise

The changes listed below tend to increase the supply of oxygen and food substances to the skeletal muscles during exercise. The blood supply to the muscles may be increased by as much as 15 times the normal. This results in blood being redirected (shunted) from the skin and digestive system to the muscles.

The circulation of the blood is increased in three ways:

1) The alternate contraction and relaxation of the muscles which surround the veins effectively pumps the venous or de-oxygenated blood back to the heart since the valves in the veins will only allow blood to flow one way.

2) As the diaphragm contracts and descends, the pressure rises in the abdomen and falls in the thorax which increases the flow of blood along the main vein from the abdomen to the heart. As the diaphragm relaxes and rises, pressure in the abdomen drops allowing the blood to flow more easily from the legs into the abdomen on its way back to the heart. The increase in rate and depth of respiration during exercise, improves the effectiveness of the pumping action of the diaphragm.

3) The increase in the volume of blood returning to the heart causes stretching of its muscle fibres. Within limits, the greater the initial length of the heart muscle fibres the more forcible the contraction which follows. There is a greater volume of blood driven out at each beat or stroke. This is coupled with an increase in the rate of heart beat, which is brought about by a complex series of nervous reflexes resulting, mainly, from an excess of carbon dioxide in the bloodstream. Although the heart is more effectively filled during exercise, it is protected from damage by a tough fibrous coat (pericardium) which surrounds it and prevents it from being overfilled.

The increase in concentration of carbon dioxide dissolved in the blood also acts on the respiratory centre in the brain causing an increase in the rate and depth of respiration, accompanied by a widening of the air passages which permit easier ventilation of the lungs.

The heat produced as a result of muscular activity is dispersed in the bloodstream and distributed to the skin, where cooling takes place so that a constant body temperature is maintained. The cooling process, obviously, occurs more quickly when the outside environment is colder, which is the normal state of affairs during swimming.

Muscles and Performance

The following provides a brief description of muscles and how they operate particularly with reference to swimming. Muscles make up about 45% of body weight and consist largely of protein. The muscles which move the body are referred to as voluntary or skeletal muscles. They are consciously controlled by the individual and are attached to bone at both ends by tendons which are very strong non-stretchable fibres. Muscle tissue is made up of many bundles of fibres which, when activated by a nervous impulse, become shorter and thicker. Each muscle fibre either contracts completely or remains at rest. Fibres cannot contract partially, but within a single muscle, some fibres may be contracted while others are relaxed. In any muscle there are always some fibres in a state of contraction. This is known as muscle tone which is a characteristic of all healthy muscles and holds them in a state of readiness for action. When these contracted fibres begin to fatigue, others will contract to maintain the tension.

Muscles usually work in groups. As one set of muscles contracts to bring about a movement, those opposing the movement relax to enable it to take place in a controlled manner. Thus, muscles which extend a limb relax, as the flexors contract to cause bending at the appropriate joint. Other muscles may be working simultaneously to prevent unwanted movements.

The performance of a novice shows a marked contrast to that of the competent swimmer. The novice uses muscles which are unnecessary for the skill and at the same time, over uses those which are essential because he has not yet acquired ability to relax the muscles opposing the required movement. This leads to energy being wasted in developing tension rather than effecting movement and it gives rise to a clumsy and uneconomical stroke or skill.

Maximum efficiency is achieved only when the appropriate muscles are used with the correct effort and all unnecessary movements are eliminated.

So that energy may be conserved and the onset of fatigue reduced, a swimmer must understand the variation in effort required for the different parts of a stroke. A competent swimmer must, therefore, learn to distinguish between the different degrees of muscular effort needed for effective performance. When a muscle, including the heart, is subjected to regular heavy exercise it responds by becoming bigger and more powerful to meet the additional demands put upon it.

Swimming in very cold water adversely affects muscular efficiency. One possible explanation for this is that the blood supply through the muscles is decreased by the cold environment and the increase in the viscosity of tissue fluid within the muscle results in reduced flow.

Relaxation

There are two kinds of relaxation, general and specific. When comparing two individuals, one may appear much more tense than the other and in consequence his movements are not so easily or so economically performed. This difference is brought about by the quality of general relaxation. Differences in general relaxation may be observed in the same individual on different occasions; a man who is normally well relaxed may, because of mental stress, ill-health or other causes, become far more tense.

Specific relaxation refers to the ability to execute a particular movement with the minimum expenditure of energy and greatest precision. Those muscles which are opposing the movement relax progressively so that a smooth action results while the muscles which prevent unwanted movement (fixators and synergists) contract just sufficiently to fulfil their functions.

When a new skill is being learned, it is inevitable that there is tension in all the muscle groups involved. As the learning process continues, the amount of unnecessary muscle work is reduced considerably. For example, when a correction is given to a beginner in the Crawl Stroke, in the point of entry of the hand, it is noticeable how stiff the arm becomes until the new action becomes habitual. It is interesting to compare the apparently effortless movements of an athlete when competing in his chosen activity with those made when he attempts a skill which is entirely foreign to him.

Better relaxation and consequent improved efficiency result from swimming progressively longer distances without stopping. Although a stroke may be quite poor technically, it can still be relaxed. Improved relaxation results in a reduction of the energy expended and so a greater distance can be swum. This in turn can lead to further improvements in technique and in relaxation.

Training

As explained earlier, during strenuous exercise the products of muscular activity build up more quickly than they can be removed or replaced. If the exercise is continued without a rest, a stage of fatigue results, making it impossible to use the affected muscles properly, performance deteriorates and cramp may occur. A period of rapid breathing will continue for some time after exercise, so that the oxygen debt may be reduced. The rate at which an individual recovers from strenuous exercise is an indication of the fitness of his cardio-vascular system (i.e., the heart, blood vessels and lungs). The trained swimmer will recover quickly and will soon be ready for more work, as is obvious in a programme based on interval training. In contrast, the untrained individual may feel distressed from unaccustomed exercise for several hours afterwards.

For training to be effective, over-loading of muscles is essential. A muscle only increases in strength and size if progressively exercised near to its limit. This is true not only of the skeletal muscles but also of the heart and the muscle fibres in the walls of blood vessels. The basis of all training schemes is systematic over-load during periods of intensive work, each of which is followed by a rest period to allow partial recovery.

The Physiological Effects on the Body produced by Swimming

All physical activity, and swimming in particular, causes short term and long term physiological effects on the body, some of which have been mentioned already. These changes are beneficial to the general health of the individual. Therefore swimming is looked upon as a health promoting activity. The short term effects occur just before and during swimming and may be summarised as follows:

a) Before swimming starts, the heart rate increases and breathing becomes deeper and more rapid in anticipation of the onset of exercise.

b) When swimming starts the pancreas and adrenal glands secrete hormones into the bloodstream which mobilise sugars to become readily available to the muscles. The much slower process of converting fats to sugars also increases.

c) As activity increases, carbon dioxide concentrations in the bloodstream increase. This high concentration triggers off the control mechanisms in the lower brain which results in increased rates of activity in the heart and in breathing. This additional activity is further stimulated by an increase in the hydrogen ion concentration of the blood, i.e. reducing the pH value or increasing acidity.

d) As exercise progresses, greater proportions of haemoglobin and plasma proteins are carried in the blood.

e) To meet the demands of the increased muscular activity, the blood vessels to the muscles increase in diameter and those to the organs, which do not play a significant part in the activity, decrease. Thus the blood supply is directed to the areas of greatest demand. Provided the water temperature is not very low, the blood vessels supplying the skin will show a net increase in diameter.

f) The pressure of the blood in the blood vessels increases to provide a greater blood flow.

g) During intense activity, perspiration will start to eliminate excess heat from the body.

The long term effects of swimming or any other exercise occur as a result of systematic but carefully monitored overloading of the body during regular performance. These benefits may be summarised as follows:

a) Swimmers are provided with a higher proportion of muscle and a lower proportion of fat than the average human being.

b) Connective tissues such as cartilage, ligaments and tendons are frequently thicker and therefore stronger.

c) The maximum volume of air of which the body can make use, is increased by increasing the tidal volume of the lungs. This results in a reduction of the number of breaths required to carry out a certain amount of work, if compared with the pre-fitness period.

d) The alveoli of the lungs receive an improved blood supply which brings about a more efficient exchange of gases.

e) The heart becomes larger and stronger and pumps a greater volume of blood on each contraction, producing a lower normal heart rate.

f) Capillaries increase in number and are found closer to muscle fibres.

g) There is an increase in the haemoglobin and number of the blood cells.

h) Muscle tissue becomes more efficient at extracting oxygen from the blood.

Chapter 3

Teaching and Learning

This chapter is intended to provide basic information and guidance on the fundamental aspects of teaching and learning, particularly for those who are comparatively new to teaching or inexperienced in its art.

In its simplest form teaching can be described as the promotion of learning, the teacher being described as the one who promotes learning in others. In this book the prime concern is with those factors which affect the quality of teaching in the fairly restricted, but rather specialised environment of the swimming pool. A good swimming teacher might be described as one who turns non-swimmers into competent swimmers, though not necessarily speed swimmers, in a reasonable period of time, using methods which make full use of natural ability and aptitude.

The Teacher

There are four qualities common to all good teachers regardless of the subject matter and these may be summarised as follows:

a) A thorough knowledge of the subject.

b) The ability to communicate at an appropriate level.

c) The ability to motivate pupils.

d) The ability to detect and meet the needs of individuals and of the group.

These basic qualities may be applied in many different ways dependent upon environment, subject matter and the ability of the pupils under tuition.

When teaching a physical skill such as swimming, the following characteristics are an essential part of a successful teacher:

a) Good preparation and planning of lessons.

b) The ability to apply theoretical knowledge to a practical situation.

c) Organisation and control of a class.

d) Good teacher/pupil relationships.

e) The ability to assess and evaluate the needs and difficulties of the individual.

The personalities of those involved in the teaching and learning process play an important part in the success of any lesson. Whilst some teachers have a natural aptitude, others can achieve success by observing successful teachers, accompanied by frequent self assessment. There is a strong body of opinion in the educational world that puts so much emphasis on the personality of the individual that it believes 'good teachers are born and not made'.

Relationships

The attitude of the teacher in relation to the class can affect its performance. This attitude can be influenced by;

a) what the teacher expects from the class,

b) the way in which the teacher may pre-judge the class or individuals in it,

c) the teacher's misconception of performance,

d) the implication that special treatment is being given to the class or to individuals within it.

Each one of these attitude factors is now considered.

a) The expectation factor

During a series of lessons a teacher will unconsciously communicate to a class or group of pupils how they are expected to behave or what standard of work is expected. In most cases a class will perform so that it meets the expectation of the teacher. Many experiments have been carried out in this area of education and the majority have provided results which support this theory. The following illustration may serve to emphasise this factor: Two groups of childen of equally mixed ability and two teachers are to carry out a particular programme. If, however, before starting the teachers are told that Group A comprises children of high ability whereas the children of Group B are of low ability, it is likely that, at the end of the teaching programme, the attainment of Group A will be better than that of Group B. This is particularly the case over a short period with a new subject or skill. Obviously, this assumes that the teachers have approximately the same experience and ability in teaching the subject concerned.

b) The pre-judgement factor

This factor is concerned with the quite natural differences in feeling which a teacher has for different classes. Most teachers (the honest ones), admit that certain classes fill them with some measure of apprehension whilst others provide a positive boost to personal morale. The pre-judgement effect is more likely to have an adverse influence on those which come into the former category. Inevitably, if a teacher feels some measure of apprehension in teaching a particular group of pupils this feeling will be communicated to the class which will in turn react to confirm the teacher's pre-judgement or prejudice. Closer investigation of the problem will usually show that, whilst the class as a whole is pre-judged by the teacher as a problem group, the basis for the pre-judgement is very often vested in a small number of individuals within the group or even a single character.

If an individual creates a disturbance within the class then the teacher may very well take it to be the signal for a much greater disturbance which is to follow and therefore react in an uncharacteristic manner by severely chastising the individual. This reaction would inevitably have some effect on the rest of the group and may very well cause within the child a feeling of being 'victimised'. If such incidents occur frequently, all members will tend, gradually, to gain the impression that they are being 'victimised' and as a consequence will tend to react in such a way that the teacher's pre-judgement becomes more and more justifiable.

c) The misconception factor

This factor is more likely to prevail in inexperienced teachers or those who work in isolation, but perhaps it should be stated that this tends to be less of a problem when teaching some form of physical activity. The misconception effect arises as a result of a teacher forming a very favourable first impression of the standard of work either of an individual or of the group as a whole. The teacher then continues to assume that the rate of progress remains the same or even improves, thus negating the need for close scrutiny of an individual or a small group within the class. During subsequent tests when performance is below expectation, the unsuspecting teacher may look upon the performance as uncharacteristic whereas, in reality, it is the test which indicates the correct level of achievement.

Nevertheless, in the swimming pool the teacher's assessment of a pupil is constantly being influenced by the pupil who, in order to take part in the lesson, has to perform in front of a teacher and provide visual evidence of progress, or lack of it.

In the swimming pool, the misconception effect can arise where a proportion of the class who are able swimmers are given a programme to follow during a lesson and the teacher assumes that all members of the group have followed the programme closely and therefore gained the appropriate level of improvement.

d) The special treatment factor

A group of pupils will often react favourably in a learning situation if they are given the impression that in some way they are getting special treatment by being allocated a favourite teacher or being provided with new swimming aids etc. The increased rate of progress of the class usually results from greater concentration in return for the special treatment received. Obviously, this reaction is made quite unconsciously by the group and is based in the psychological reactions of individuals. It is not likely that the special treatment factor will play a major part with any single group of pupils in a swimming pool, since the number of opportunities when it may be employed is very limited, particularly where the class is seen only once a week for a comparatively short period of time.

Communication

Ultimately, the principal characteristic of a successful teacher is the ability to communicate effectively with a class and the most effective methods of communication in the teaching of swimming are likely to be, *visual, verbal and manual*.

Visual

Since children learn by observation and imitation, a good demonstration with appropriate brief comment will help to give a clear idea of the skill to be learned. It is important that the pupils are given the opportunity to watch a good performance in the water whilst the more important factors are being emphasised by the teacher on the pool-side. An important aspect of visual communication is the use of mime and body signals which can save wear and tear of the voice. It goes without saying, however, that any demonstration which the teacher makes on the pool-side must have accuracy.

Verbal

It is important to give verbal guidance during the teaching process in order to reinforce the demonstration. To be effective, the verbal guidance should be brief and relevant. Talking about a swimming stroke before it has been seen is likely to be useless and possibly confusing.

Teaching points are needed for every practice and every repeated practice. Pupils are likely to learn best when they can focus on the major points and therefore concentrate on them. Concentration on one teaching point at a time will tend to avoid confusion. It is important that, whilst the pupils are in the environment of the swimming pool and have access to the water, a far higher proportion of the lesson should be spent by the pupils practising rather than by the teacher explaining to them what is to be done. Whenever communication is being reinforced by verbal guidance, it is important that the guidance should be positive rather than negative. For example, when teaching the Front Crawl, an instruction such as 'right elbow higher' is much more direct and useful to the pupil than 'don't keep your right elbow so close to the water'.

Manual

In the case of some children it may be necessary for their limbs to be guided through the correct pathway of a movement required in a stroke. This has the disadvantage, however, that the learner gains little or no appreciation of the forces which have to be applied at various stages of the movement and, for maximum benefit, the teacher needs to be in the water. Therefore manual guidance should be used sparingly and mainly as a corrective measure, when other methods have failed. In any case, practice of the appropriate skill should follow immediately.

Acquisition of Skill

The definitions of skill are as numerous as the number of skills since each one requires a different series of actions. Here, however, it is sufficient to refer to them as 'an economic and efficient organisation of action responses which achieve a pre-determined effect'. The skills of swimming are achieved through a series of co-ordinated movements which must take place in a set order. It will be readily appreciated that if the movements of individual limbs are correct but are not co-ordinated in the correct sequence, then the pupil will not be a competent swimmer. When a pupil attempts the first rudimentary movements of swimming it is likely that he or she will perform unnecessary actions. It is important, with the help of the teacher, to eliminate these immediately, so that adaptation to the correct actions can be made as early as possible. For example, this can be particularly important for children learning Breast Stroke since it is the opinion of many experienced swimming teachers that 'screw kicks' often arise from confused or inaccurate teaching of the stroke at the formative stage. If faults are allowed to persist, it becomes increasingly difficult to eliminate them later.

When learning a skill, 'feed-back' is particularly important since learners need to be constantly reassured that their performances are improving along the right lines. Therefore they should be reminded of their progress regularly. The emphasis should always be on praise and positive reinforcement. Adverse criticism of genuine attempts to carry out the teacher's wishes should be extremely rare and made only in a friendly helpful manner.

Motivation

Motivation is an extremely important factor when learning any skill. For maximum success in the rather strange environment of the swimming pool, the pupils must really 'want' to acquire the skill being taught. It is likely that the teacher will best motivate beginners by providing an opportunity for individuals to select the type of stroke most suited to their natural endowment. Such a course of action is more likely to produce earlier success. This is why there is general support for the multi-stroke method of teaching non-swimmers.

Since early success generates motivation, it is important to get any pupil moving through the water as soon as possible regardless of any inaccuracies in the initial stroke technique. Early success will serve to produce greater desire for better swimming. It is universally appreciated that motivation drops when progress stagnates. For the younger child particularly, the possibility of an award can provide an added boost and therefore full advantage should be taken of the ASA/ESSA Award Schemes in addition to any simple challenges devised by the teacher.

The majority of children thrive on some form of competition and therefore motivation is likely to be increased if a competitive element can be introduced into the lessons. However, there are children who are adversely affected by a competitive element and in classes where this arises, attempts should be made to introduce alternative inducement. This reaction to competition is dependent to a large extent on personality, since some children can cope with the additional stress and anxiety much better than others.

The need for constant motivation is even greater for competitive swimmers since they must devote a large proportion of their free time to the sport.

Though regular and frequent practice is an important part of learning a skill, boredom and fatigue may quickly develop if too much time is spent on a single activity or practice. Once interest is lost, it is not easily regained. For this reason the content of a lesson and the way in which it is presented should be looked upon as important factors in maintaining the interest and enjoyment of the pupils.

Teaching Method – Whole Part Whole

Good stroke technique requires a series of actions to be correctly co-ordinated. Teaching may proceed by a concentration on the component parts of a stroke before attempting to co-ordinate them as a whole. It may begin with an initial attempt at the whole stroke with subsequent part practices, as a means of correction and consolidation. Points can be made for both approaches but it is generally accepted that the latter is better. It is possible to swim strokes without a complete awareness of the precise actions required. Therefore, following a demonstration, with appropriate commentary, pupils are encouraged to attempt their own interpretations of the stroke required. Early efforts may be crude but a feeling for the whole movement will be gained. Thereafter, one part of the stroke is practised and followed by the consolidation of this additional skill, in another attempt at the whole stroke. The sequence of whole stroke, part practice, whole stroke, is continued until a degree of competence is achieved. This process should normally feature in most lessons.

Learning

Having considered some of the more important aspects involved in teaching, it is just as important to develop an insight into some of the more elementary factors involved in the learning process. An experienced teacher will readily appreciate that pupils learn at different rates and therefore as far as possible pupils within a class should be treated as individuals. Since swimming involves movements of all parts of the body, particularly the limbs, the

physical structure of an individual will affect the rate of progress towards competence. As in the case of the teacher, the pupils' personalities play a large part in the rate at which they learn. In general terms, personalities fall into two categories, introvert and extrovert, although it must be appreciated that the personality of every individual is really a mixture of these two factors, even though, in many cases, one is more dominant than the other. In general, persons with introverted personalities will tend to take comfort from having others around who are doing exactly the same, whilst those with extrovert personalities will tend to spend time drawing attention to their individualities. In the eye of an inexperienced teacher, the extrovert pupil might easily be mistaken for one who frequently misbehaves. The rate of learning is different for each individual and the effective teacher should adopt an approach which is beneficial to the majority of the class. However, individuals within the class may have to be given special attention at various stages during the learning process. Therefore, it is important for the teacher to appreciate the reasons why communication might break down. Such an understanding may well prevent problems arising during lessons.

There are five major sources for communication breakdown as follows:

Saturation
This refers to the saturation of the pupils' capacity to cope with any more information than that already provided. This will depend on factors such as physical capacity, previous experience and a general standard of intelligence.

Distractions
These may be internal and external. The latter are generally within the control of the teacher but, internal distractions, such as fear or apprehension, may require a great deal of skill on the part of the teacher if they are not to pass unnoticed and consequently, adversely affect the rate of learning.

Confusing Presentation
This refers to the information being given to the pupils. The vocabulary used must be within the knowledge and experience of the pupils and to be effective, all instructions and descriptions should be brief and relevant.

Implied Assumptions
It is not uncommon for some teachers to assume that pupils will automatically understand information presented to them. For example, it is not unknown for a teacher when describing the arm action of Front Crawl, to refer to the 'catch position' without first describing precisely what it is. This example also serves to emphasise the danger of using undefined terms as in the case of the word 'catch'.

Mis-interpretation
Individuals, especially young children with limited experience, may mis-interpret any instructions simply because they have not had experience of the particular format in which they are presented. Therefore, the teacher on the pool-side should constantly check that instructions are being understood.

This chapter has attempted to introduce some of the important factors which affect the teaching and learning processes as applied to a skill such as swimming. Inevitably, it has not been possible to deal in depth with any particular aspect but those wishing to pursue the subject further may care to consult one or more of the large number of publications devoted entirely to it.

Reader's notes

Chapter 4

The Practice of Teaching

This chapter has been prepared mainly for the benefit of teachers working with classes of about 20 pupils.

It is hoped, however, that the teacher with only one or two pupils will also find much that is of value, as the principles of teaching are a common factor in all situations.

Some children are quick to learn and may be able to swim for the first time shortly after entering the water; others may require a long period of patient help and encouragement before attempting their first strokes. It is important, therefore, that the maximum and most efficient use should be made of the facilities and time available and every effort should be made to get the pupils swimming as soon as possible. Children are motivated by success and the earlier they become waterborne and achieve movement through the water, the sooner they will swim efficiently. Lessons should always be carefully prepared, learning situations should be made as interesting and enjoyable as possible and early teaching should be kept simple and free from complicated requirements of technique.

General Considerations

Use of Time and Facilities
For the most effective teaching, exclusive use of the swimming pool is desirable. This also allows for greater numbers to take part.

The main aim is to get children swimming as soon as possible, and preferably as young as possible. Where there are school pools children have regular opportunities to swim without having to travel. Furthermore, additional swimming programmes can be provided out of school time. Most school swimming lessons, however, are carried out in public pools with consequent limitations in terms of availability of water space and the need to travel. It is important, therefore, when devising programmes, to include those groups which are likely to derive most benefit, all things considered. By using these, many small groups of children can and do, have a regular opportunity to swim, without having to travel a great distance. Furthermore, additional swimming lessons can be provided out of school time.

In addition to lessons for beginners, it is desirable also, to provide opportunities for swimmers to improve personal performances and to derive full benefit from such activity as part of a physical education and swimming club programme.

Not to be forgotten are the slow learners, some of whom are to be found in every class. Every effort should be made to provide further opportunites for these children, preferably with special arrangements, whereby a confident person is actually in the water, giving help and support.

The length of lessons will vary with the abilities of classes. It is felt that between 20 and 30 minutes is adequate for learners, but for more able groups, lessons might last for 45 minutes, especially if they are working on other activities, such as survival swimming.

Where dressing room facilities permit, one class should be ready to enter the water as the previous class leaves. It is wasteful of valuable water time to have the pool empty for long periods while classes are changing over.

Environment Conducive to Learning

Water Temperature
The temperature of the water and the air temperature will play a large part in determining the pace and duration of the lesson. Ideally, the water temperature should be at 27°C(80°F). For comfort on the pool-side and to avoid condensation, the air temperature should be slightly higher. Conditions prevailing outdoors are rarely ideal. Even in mid-summer, outdoor water temperatures are often below 16°C(60°F), in which case the teacher must consider carefully the advisability of putting pupils into the water at all.

There is a strong link between water temperature and success in learning to swim. The warmer the water and the more comfortable the environment, the easier it is to concentrate attention on the task. In cold water, the lessons should be of very short duration at the start (even as short as five minutes for very young beginners), gradually lengthening in time as acclimatisation takes place. The pace of these lessons must be lively, involving as much continuous movement as possible, and so devised that the pupil may keep his shoulders under the water surface at all times. Lesson planning and organisation must be such that there is no waste of time. A towel and warm clothing should be close at hand for the end of the lesson.

Size of Class
It is impossible to provide for every situation in determining the size of a class. Inevitable, this is linked with the school, club or pool organisation, the ages and abilities of the pupils, the size of the pool and depth of water available and the use of transport between school and pool. Generally speaking, there should be at least one teacher to every 20 pupils, but with very young children a smaller ratio is desirable. At all times when pupils are

in the water, a competent life saver should be present, able and ready to act in emergency. Only the teacher can decide, in the light of prevailing circumstances, how the class should be organised. Experience has shown that, all things considered, the level of learning is higher when a block system of lessons is used, e.g. 15 lessons spread over three weeks are more beneficial than 15 lessons spread over 15 weeks.

Suitability of the Pool
The shape of the pool and the depth of water are factors which should be considered in relation to the size and ability of the class and the type of lesson to be taught. In the majority of swimming pools, most of the learning is carried out across the width of the pool. This, however, is not the only way in which water space may be used and organisation should be flexible. By using different formations or sometimes using ropes to mark off water areas, the pool space can be adapted to suit the needs of the class as a whole, ability groups within the class, or to allow for a variety of activities which the teacher might wish to include in the lesson.

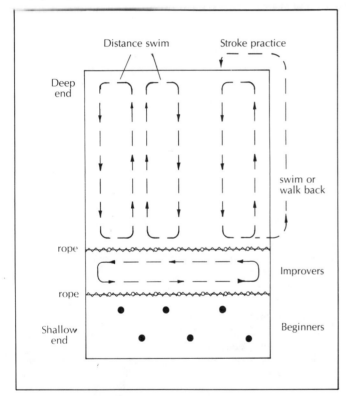

Fig. 4·1 (a) ELEMENTARY CLASS
Varied strokes/Four Groups/Varied activities

In working across the pool, it is obviously advisable to have the best swimmers at the deep end ranging in ability to the beginners at the shallow end. Such an arrangement should apply to class and group work.

Where space is limited, pupils can be arranged in pairs, working in waves. One sets off and having reached about half way across, is followed by his partner in the same track. On reaching the opposite side of the pool, number one waits until his partner has joined him before setting off again. Thus, each works at his own pace with a fairly long, clear space ahead. If space is limited children can work in a similar fashion in groups of three.

The area of shallow water available is very important and where this is limited it becomes necessary to make use of deeper water. This may necessitate the careful and controlled use of aids (see Chapter 5, Teaching Beginners).

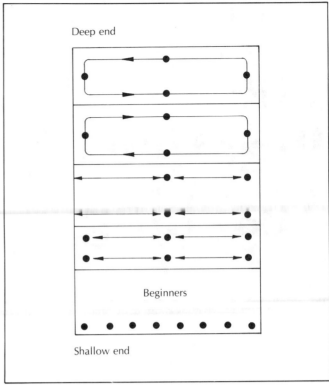

Fig. 4·1 (b) MIXED ACTIVITIES
Five Groups (with or without ropes)

More advanced and interesting activities can be attempted such as diving, survival activities, life saving and ball games, when careful thought is given to preparation and use of space.

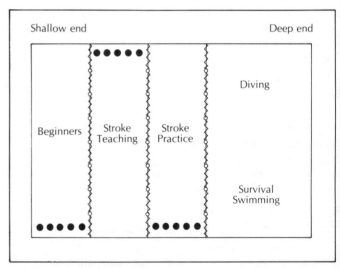

Fig. 4·2 MIXED ACTIVITIES
Five Groups (with or without ropes)

Safety

Obviously a swimming pool is a place of potential danger and the teacher must take every precaution to minimise this, without being over-restrictive. Certain rules and routines must be established, leading to acceptable behaviour by the class:

a) Good discipline must be observed at all times.

b) No pupil should be allowed in the water until the teacher has given permission.

c) No running along the pool-side or pushing others into the water should be allowed.

d) Signals should be obeyed promptly, especially those indicating stopping and getting out of the water.

e) The number of pupils in the class should be checked from time to time, and particularly, at the end of the lesson.

f) Long poles should be placed on both sides of the pool, for use in cases of emergency.

g) A rope should be used showing the limit of shallow water appropriate for the class.

h) In large pools and open water, it is often advisable to distinguish non-swimmers by the use of coloured caps.

i) In open water, rivers, or crowded swimming pools, a system whereby paired swimmers are always aware of each other, is advisable.

j) Floats and other aids are valuable assets in learning to swim, but they should be used under the direction of the teacher and in a safe depth of water.

k) When diving is in progress, it is desirable to mark off the area by means of a rope. Care must be taken by divers to ensure that the entry area is clear of swimmers and the water is sufficiently deep. Swimmers should not be permitted to swim near or under diving boards.

l) The teacher should have a sound working knowledge of efficient methods of resuscitation, particularly the expired air method. He should also be acquainted with the normal emergency arrangements provided at the pool, and locations of first aid equipment and telephone.

m) Strict supervision should be exercised while children are using changing accommodation and no children should be allowed near the water unless supervised. School pools should always be locked when not in use.

n) For effective teaching, as well as safety, the teacher's place during the lesson should be on the pool-side. For demonstrations in the water, a pupil should be used, with the rest of the class watching. Should the teacher feel the need for himself to give support in the water to a timorous or small beginner, he should do so at some specially arranged time outside the lesson, in a one to one situation.

o) Sweets and chewing gum should not be allowed in the pool. It is dangerous to enter the water with these in the mouth.

p) Swim hats should be worn by all pupils with long hair, or the hair should be tied safely, so that it cannot cover the face and especially the mouth.

Hygiene

Pupils should be trained to play their part in keeping the swimming pool clean. Clothing should be arranged tidily in cubicles or baskets. The use of a handkerchief, toilet, showers and footbath should be an essential part of preparation for the lesson. Pupils suffering from catarrh, sore throat, foot infection or any kind of open sore should be excluded from swimming. Regular foot and cleanliness inspections should be carried out before classes enter the water. Swim-wear should be washed after use as this may become dirty thus providing a source of a infection. Walking along the pool-side in outdoor shoes should not be permitted. After each swim pupils should dry themselves thoroughly, giving particular attention to hair, ears and feet.

Equipment

Aids to Floatation
A variety of these should be available in adequate number to provide at least one for each pupil and they should be ready, on the pool-side, at the start of each lesson.

Ropes
Ideally, these should be available in different lengths so that the pool can be divided into areas of various sizes and shapes, according to the requirements of the lesson to be presented. Where possible, small floats should be attached to them, at intervals, unless floating plastic rope is used.

Clocks
Every pool should have a large clock with a sweephand indicating seconds. Where one of these is not available, a number of smaller clocks can be sealed in plastic bags and placed at suitable points around the pool. The main use of these clocks is for the Interval Method of training, for the timing of Schedules, or Time-Distance Swims.

Notice Board
This should be kept up to date with details of teams, tests and items of interest.

Blackboards
These can be used to indicate assignments of work during schedule lessons or for the group work included in an orthodox type lesson. They should be placed around the pool, so that detail may be easily read by pupils from their positions in the water.

Wall Charts
A brief reference to an illustration is a useful supplement to an explanation or demonstration. Wall charts used for this purpose should be waterproofed and displayed neatly, preferably on wall boards especially provided for the purpose.

Games Equipment
Plastic hoops, table tennis balls, playballs, rubber bricks, plastic braid in various colours, are all useful pieces of equipment which can be used for training and recreational purposes.

Teaching Technique

The Teacher
Just as it is accepted that children differ from each other, so do teachers who are individuals with their own talents and personalities. It is unwise, therefore, to be dogmatic about teaching procedures and systems. Teachers must assess their own capabilities and organise lessons accordingly. There are, however, some general principles which should apply.

For success in any lesson, it is essential that a good teacher-pupil relationship is established from the beginning. The teacher's appearance should be clean, smart and appropriate to the pool-side situation. The work should be presented in a clear, patient and amiable manner.

In a swimming pool there is a need for control with a firm attitude towards safety regulations, but at the same time the teacher should show patience and understanding. A self-imposed discipline by the pupils, based on mutual respect and confidence, is preferable and should be developed. A noisy teacher will not gain the confidence of beginners.

It is important in gaining the confidence of pupils for the teacher to communicate individually with each one during every lesson.

Teaching Position and Use of Voice
At all times the teacher should take account of his position in relation to the group he is addressing. The best position will depend upon the size and disposition of the class and the acoustics of the pool. With small numbers, a semi-circle facing the teacher, whose attention is transferred to all members in the group will give good rapport and a feeling of individual association. On the other hand, with large numbers spread down the length of the pool, the teacher's best position is at one end,

standing far enough in front of the line of pupils for each to see and hear him (fig. 4·3).

It is essential that all explanations and comments are heard clearly by the whole class. Acoustics in swimming pools are often bad and raising the voice, does not always overcome this problem. Teaching in a monotone becomes boring and ineffective, so the pitch should be varied with emphasis placed on the more important points.

When detailed explanations are necessary pupils should be called to pre-arranged demonstration positions in which it will be possible for the teacher to be heard, using a normal speaking voice. Speech should be delivered slowly and deliberately, thus allowing everything to be heard.

Demonstrations indicating limb movements, given by the teacher on the pool-side, can be most useful at times. It is important that they should be accurate and shown from various viewpoints so that pupils may not only see, but also understand the teaching points. It should be realised also, that a demonstration given whilst facing the pupils can sometimes be difficult to interpret.

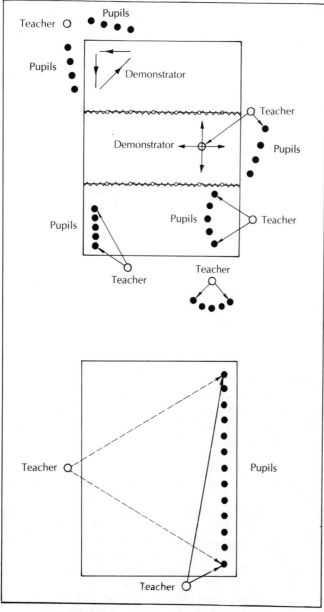

Fig. 4·3 TEACHING POSITIONS

A whistle must be used sparingly in order to be effective. Its use should mean STOP, LOOK and LISTEN. The class reaction should be immediate after only one blast, which should be sharp and loud enough to arrest attention. Before speaking, the teacher should ensure that the class is ready to listen.

Team Teaching
By arrangement, one person is appointed in overall charge of a group of assistant teachers, who are themselves made responsible for a specific number of pupils. This senior teacher must have the authority to take general control of the session, perhaps, at times to teach the whole class, setting the activities to be practised and indicating when these should be changed. The assistant teachers each direct their own groups, making individual corrections and modifications where necessary.

Teaching the Strokes
Multi Stroke Approach
Once they can move in the water the pupils will wish to learn how to modify their initial exploratory activities and how to perform movements which will provide more efficient propulsion.

Preference is often expressed for one of the main strokes. Breast Stroke has obvious use in endurance swimming and life saving, and it is often claimed that if it is to be taught at all, it should be taught first, thus eliminating the likelihood of a screw kick. On the other hand, Front Crawl is said to be a more natural movement, closely resembling the limb action of normal walking. Others contend that swimming on the back should be taught first, as this reduces the possibly frightening experience of water splashing over the face; furthermore, the pupil is able to breathe easily and see the teacher at all times, thus feeling reassured and confident.

Whatever the merits of any one stroke, it is preferable, in the early stages, to use a multi stroke approach, whereby pupils are given an opportunity to experience them all. Following a quick and simple introduction to the propulsive movements of each of the strokes, with emphasis on the leg action, each pupil is allowed to choose and to practise the one which gives him most success in moving through the water.

Stroke Development
Once the pupils can swim across the width of the pool using their chosen strokes, they should now be taught the basic actions of the various strokes. This may be done by providing opportunities, in each lesson, for the whole class to concentrate on one particular stroke. Initially, the practices should be of short duration, gradually increasing in length, until the lesson may have as its main section the development of one particular stroke with opportunity also for the individual's favourite stroke to be practised.

It is emphasised that the pupils should be able to glide through the water in prone and supine positions and to regain standing positions before attempting the actions of the strokes.

When teaching the strokes the following procedure has been found, generally, to be the most successful:

a) Demonstration of the complete stroke, with commentary by the teacher.

b) Pupils attempt the complete stroke.

c) Attention is focused on the legs. From the horizontal gliding position, prone or supine and holding floats in support, the pupils attempt to propel themselves further with the leg kick, which should begin as the momentum of the glide is finishing. The teacher directs the efforts with appropriate comments.

d) To instil a visual image, a demonstration of the leg kick is given by a reasonably successful pupil.

e) Others try to copy.

f) As soon as the pupils can achieve a reasonable leg kick to enable them to maintain balance and propulsion, arm movements can be incorporated. Directions for these movements should be simple and quickly given, e.g.'pull, push, lift, recover' for Front Crawl: 'press, bend, forward, reach' for Breast Stroke. Accompanied by demonstrations, such general directions as these are quite adequate at this stage. The teacher should move around helping individuals or small groups working on their chosen strokes. While some children will achieve success immediately, others will be less successful and may find it helpful to practise the leg action while holding the pool rail. Such practice, however, should be of short duration. The teacher should encourage every pupil to increase distances, at the same time emphasising the need to maintain reasonable technique.

Lesson Forms

Each swimming lesson should be part of a plan or scheme of work designed to provide a comprehensive education in swimming. Whatever the activities chosen or the stage reached, every lesson should be properly prepared in outline, taking into consideration the facilities available and the level of abilities in the class. Each lesson should have an aim which is quite clear and easily understood by the class. The lesson should consist of a variety of purposeful activities, presented in an interesting and stimulating fashion. While it should be demanding, it should be within the capabilities of all the pupils, thus presenting a challenge resulting in a sense of achievement. There are several lesson forms whereby a scheme of work can be carried out.

The Orthodox Teaching Lesson

In this lesson the fundamental swimming skills are taught as a class activity and then practised in ability groups. However, there may be times when the class activity might be continued throughout the lesson. On occasions, with a class of mixed ability the lesson might begin with the pupils proceeding to their pre-arranged group places and continuing with work already assigned by the teacher, or continuing the lesson from the point at which the previous one finished. This last arrangement would leave the teacher free to start teaching with the group most in need of particular attention. There may be times when a return from group work to class activity may be made in order to correct a common error.

The lesson should have periods of fairly intense work interspersed with short periods of explanation or appropriate demonstration. It should be emphasized, however, that watching and listening should not unduly limit the essential amount of practice.

The following Lesson Plan can be adapted for most orthodox lessons (time 20-25 minutes):

a) Explanation of Lesson Aim (1-2 minutes).
This should be related to what has been done before, or it should follow the use of visual aids or a demonstration by an able performer, if a new aspect is to be introduced. The time spent should be short and the explanation clearly presented.

b) Entry and Warm-up or Introductory Activity (1-2 minutes).
The tone and tempo of the lesson can be set here. By presenting a stimulating activity the teacher can often succeed in catching, immediately, the interest and enthusiasm of the pupils.

c) The Main Section (10-12 minutes).
This may consist of a short revision of previous work followed by an extension and development of the same activity. On the other hand, an entirely new activity may be taught.

The following procedure has been found effective:

i) A quick demonstration with appropriate teaching points.

ii) Attempts at the whole skill with hints and comments to class and individuals.

iii) A breakdown of the whole skill with repeated practices of parts of it, interspersed with comments and teaching points by the teacher.

iv) A final return to the whole skill.
This procedure may be carried out as a class activity for the whole of the time or it might occupy only part of the time, then followed by further practices in ability groups.

d) Contrasting Activity (3-5 minutes).
Revision of strokes. Diving activities. Survival practices. Such skills might be included as a class activity or with the class arranged in ability groups all practising the same skill, or with each group practising a different activity.

e) Supervised Free Practice (2-4 minutes).
Here the class may practise any purposeful self-chosen activity. There is general supervision by the teacher but no formal instruction.

Group Work

Most classes display a wide range of proficiency which can be reasonably well accommodated by arranging the pupils in two, three or even four ability groups. On occasions it is advantageous for a class of a wide range of ability to work as a unit with the teacher directing the activity. Apart from the basic teaching of the main work of the lesson, this arrangement gives the teacher the opportunity to establish certain routines, and systems of control, e.g., the use of whistle signals, methods of using floats, organisation of partner work. Then follows practice in groups at varying levels of ability, the teacher giving attention where it is most needed, either to basic teaching or to more advanced development of the work in hand.

Assignments of work for each of the groups may be given verbally, posted on boards or written on sheets of paper placed around the pool-side, in positions from which they can be read by the pupils from their places in the water. Group work may be included at any stage during the lesson;

a) as a continuation of the main section of the lesson, following the teaching of basic work as a class activity,

b) contrasting activities, following the main section of the lesson, may be carried out in groups, or

c) a lesson may begin with the class arranged in groups, continuing the work of the previous lesson, to be followed later by class teaching in another aspect of swimming.

Suggested Layout Of Lesson Plan

SCHOOL/CLASS:　　　　　　　　NO. OF PUPILS:　　　　　　　AGE RANGE OF PUPILS:

WATER TIME:　　　　　　　　　POOL CONDITIONS:　　　　　　EQUIPMENT:

ABILITY OF PUPILS:

OBJECTIVE/THEME:

INTRODUCTORY ACTIVITIES:

MAIN THEME ACTIVITIES:

GROUP WORK

GROUP 1		GROUP 2		GROUP 3	
Practical	T.P.	Practical	T.P.	Practical	T.P.

CONTRASTING ACTIVITY

GROUP 1	GROUP 2	GROUP 3

Note

The number of groups depends on abilities of pupils, space available and the variety of work to be developed.
This example shows three groups. A schedule may be included. On occasions the class may be treated as a single group.

SUPERVISED FREE PRACTICE:

PTO　　　　　(a)　　　　Evaluation of lesson　　　　(b)　　　　Observations for action in next lesson

This provides a typical plan for the preparation of an orthodox lesson. A conscientious teacher will prepare a lesson using such a format and keep continuous records. Sufficient flexibility should be allowed within its general structure to allow variation from time to time so that the needs of the pupils can be fulfilled.

Schedule lesson

Length of lesson = 30 minutes — width of pool 12.5 metres　　　　Rest 1 minute after each section

STROKE	WIDTHS PER GROUP			DETAIL
	A	B	C	
Free Choice – Full Stroke	8	6	4	All groups start at easy pace then try to swim succeeding widths with fewer strokes.
Front Crawl – Full Stroke	8	6	4	A concentrate on long stroking. B concentrate on correct arm entry. C concentrate on smooth action.
Front Crawl – Leg Action	6	4	2	All groups holding floats – emphasise up-kick
Front Crawl – Full Stroke	10	6	4	All groups concentrate on the kicking action.
Stroke-Swimming	12	8	4	A swim 3 stroke medley – changing stroke each width. B Swim 2 stroke medley – changing stroke each width. C Swim 2nd choice stroke – concentration on leg action.
No 1 Choice – Full Stroke	6	6	2	All groups concentrate on breathing OUT.
No 1 Choice – Legs Only	4	4	2	All groups kick HARD.
No 1 Choice – Full Stroke	4	4	4	All groups swim EASY.
	4	4	2	All groups swim alternate HARD-EASY.
	4	2	2	All groups swim HARD.
Total metres	825	625	375	

The Stroke Schedule Lesson

Having used orthodox lessons to teach fundamental swimming skills, some opportunity should be given for more intensive practice of them. This can be provided by using a schedule type lesson whereby each of the ability groups already mentioned, is given an assignment of work which will occupy almost the whole of the time. Classes will already be accustomed to working in groups to carry out set work as part of the orthodox lesson, so they will be familiar with the general organisation (fig. 4·4).

The schedule lesson should not be regarded as an easy option. It should be used only occasionally at the termination of a series of lessons. The pupils should be fully extended and apart from the work to be done on the pool-side during the lesson, the teacher must give a great deal of thought to the preparation of schedules. It is not sufficient to present the same work for each group with variations in distance only. It is assumed that there will be a definite knowledge of the basic skills of the strokes and the work should be selected, specifically, to improve particular aspects of the strokes, as required, and in accordance with the differing abilities of the groups. Points to be stressed should be indicated verbally or preferably in writing on schedule boards, or on sheets of paper. While the work is being carried out the teacher should be moving around, ensuring that all pupils are working and that the schedules are understood. Pupils may be selected for individual attention or it may be necessary to deal with a whole group. Occasionally, the work of all groups might be suspended in order to stress a point of technique applicable to the whole class. As in all lesson forms, some flexibility should be allowed, to suit the occasion.

In preparing schedules the teacher should consider and include activities to provide for the following:

a) Improvement of technique.

b) Improvement of stamina – also related to technique.

c) Versatility and variety of strokes.

d) Making the work progressive by including more work than in previous lessons.

e) Variations in presentation, e.g., working on a time basis allowing so many minutes on each stroke section. This requires a large clock which all can see, or a change-over controlled by whistle.

f) Different strokes for each group.

g) Work to be made progressively more demanding by reducing the rest taken between repetitions; increasing the number of repetitions; increasing the speed of each repetition; by attempting combinations of these.

Schedules of work can be written on blackboards, placed at convenient points around the pool-side, on sheets of paper pinned on small portable boards, or written in water-proof ink on sheets of paper, dampened and placed on the pool edge.

An example of a simple schedule lesson is set out opposite. Here there are three ability groups, ranged along the pool-side, working in widths. Groups may also work in lengths.

It is not usually sufficient to arrange schedules by merely considering the numbers of widths to be swum. Other aspects need to be considered and modifications must always be necessary to suit the ability levels of the groups.

In accordance with the development of the programme the

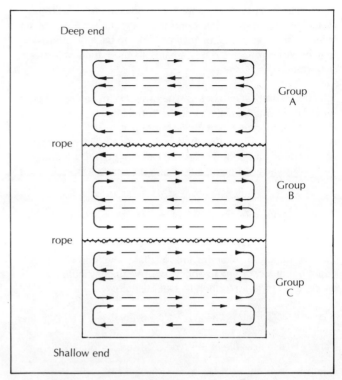

Fig.4.4 STROKE SCHEDULE LESSON
Chain swimming – direction of progress being alternately clockwise and anti-clockwise to avoid collision

teacher may introduce variations as the following three examples indicate:

Lesson	Group A	Group B	Group C
a)	Front Crawl	Breast Stroke	Back Crawl
b)	Four Strokes	Three Strokes	Two Strokes
c)	Survival swimming in clothes	Two Strokes	One stroke, with or without aids

As performance improves, it may be appropriate to include some practices with arms only, for the most advanced swimmers. It is emphasised that the schedule lesson is used for development and practice of strokes. It should not be confused with the orthodox teaching lesson in which the class may be divided into ability groups, one of which might be given a stroke schedule to perform.

The Time/Distance Lesson

This lesson presents the Challenge or the Test. No specific teaching is involved but first-class organisation is essential. Having taught the skills of swimming and having provided opportunities for practising and improving them, using the two types of lesson forms already mentioned, it is desirable that pupils should be given the opportunity to test their own progress. Generally speaking, there are two main criteria of progress:

a) The ability to swim for a longer period or a longer distance without stopping.

b) The ability to cover a set distance in a faster time.

It may be said that the first of these measures is an increase in the individual's endurance, while the second measures an improvement in efficiency. In orthodox and stroke schedule lessons the teacher should be aiming to achieve both. This lesson, provides an opportunity for these to be assessed. Testing without teaching and development is of little value, so this form of lesson should be used very sparingly, perhaps once per month.

The teacher may wish to impose conditions in the swim by stipulating that it should be done in a particular way, e.g. on the front, on the back, or changing from front to back on alternate lengths. Attention should be primarily focused upon objective performance.

Initially, a short version of this type of swim can be carried out in widths or in small circles, using the normal three group system, with an appropriate target for each group, e.g. A–3 minutes, B–2 minutes, C–1 minute. It might even be used as a contrasting activity during an orthodox lesson. Later, more difficult and complex swims can be organised and the whole lesson devoted to them.

As soon as possible, the length of the pool should be used and the 'chain' system of swimming adopted.

With 20 minutes' swimming time available the following targets might be set, according to ability, but swimmers should be encouraged to swim further, if at all possible.

Group A – 500 metres   Group B – 300 metres   Group C – 200 metres

Variety is also possible in this type of lesson, as follows:

Group A	Group B	Group C
Breast Stroke-survival swim in clothes	Front Crawl – distance swim in a given time	Various strokes specified – time taken for a given distance.

Ideally, when these tests have been carried out, the results should be posted on the notice board together with the previous test results. In this way each child can gauge his own progress and be stimulated to greater effort.

The Recreational Lesson

This type of lesson, which should be given occasionally, includes a variety of games and purposeful aquatic activities. In the early stages, these should be informal and of a general play nature.

Activities with hoops and small balls, collecting objects from the bottom of the pool, tag games and similar activities might occupy the last part of an orthodox lesson. Later, more sophisticated activities can be introduced and presented in the form of a complete lesson which could include relay races, improvised games in small groups, water polo, survival swimming activities, recreative partner activities and synchronised swimming skills.

For further information see Chapter 13.

Syllabus

An ideal syllabus for a school or club should be as comprehensive as possible in an attempt to cater for all levels of ability and aptitude. It will be determined by many factors which include:

a) Facilities and time available.

b) The number of teachers and helpers available and their abilities to teach swimming.

c) The ability of the pupils.

d) The tradition existing in the school or club.

e) The personal requirements of members of adult and club groups.

The main aim should be to help each person to become a swimmer for the purpose of saving life in water, should the occasion arise, and to enjoy the recreational aspects of swimming. This suggests the need to include:

a) Teaching beginners to swim.

b) Teaching the main strokes.

c) Teaching other strokes such as Side Stroke or Back Stroke with circular kick.

d) Diving, to the stages of Plunge Dive and Plain Header. Spring board and firm board diving can be included where facilities exist.

e) Survival swimming and Life Saving should be introduced at an early stage in an informal but objective way. These activities can be developed until pupils are ready to prepare for various tests and awards.

f) Water games and swimming stunts should be included from the earliest stages. They are useful for variation, and the development of versatility in the water.

g) Competitive skills such as starts, turns and relay take-overs may be introduced for the more able swimmers.

h) Water polo.

i) Synchronised swimming.

Awards should be regarded as additional to the whole scheme of work and they should not assume undue importance. They are valuable as a means of maintaining interest and measuring achievement for those with ability, but they should not over-influence the swimming curriculum as a whole.

One particular risk to take guard against is that of misusing enthusiasm by allowing very young swimmers to spend undue time in the water to cover long distances.

Almost as important as the preparation of a swimming programme, is an assessment of its effectiveness which will probably result in modifications from time to time. Therefore, it is necessary to keep records of lesson plans with evaluations of their effectiveness.

Reader's notes

Reader's notes

Chapter 5

Teaching Beginners

In the chapter on Teaching and Learning, stress was placed on the role of the teacher and the need to appreciate that since pupils learn at different rates they should, as far as possible, be treated as individuals.

Success in learning depends to a large extent on the development of a sound pupil-teacher relationship. The pupil who admires and respects the teacher will want to try to please by following any instructions given as well as possible. If, in turn, the teacher presents the work in a clear, patient and amiable manner and grades the work to be done, pupils will be inspired with confidence.

Initially, the teacher's task will be to help pupils to feel at home in the water and to gain confidence through finding that learning to swim can be a pleasurable experience. It must be remembered that adjusting the body to a medium which not only counteracts the force of gravity but also has an unstable base can cause problems of balance with non-swimmers. Movement in water will be strange to most of the pupils and their initial experiences will largely determine whether or not a swimming lesson proves to be an enjoyable occasion.

For that reason early lessons should be short, in shallow water at a comfortable temperature and a warm air temperature. Ideally, lessons with beginners should be in learner pools where they have exclusive use of the water space. The sooner the pupils discover that water will support the body and that movements of limbs can propel the body through the water, the greater the chance that they will learn to swim quickly and with confidence.

To enable pupils to develop confidence in the teacher and in the learning situation, the teaching approach must be carefully considered. The following points should help to establish a good learning atmosphere:

a) The presentation of the activities and the activities themselves must be enjoyable.

b) The teaching style should convey competence, concern for individuals and enthusiasm.

c) The pupils should be fully involved in the learning situation. They should understand the purpose of the practices which they are asked to undertake and helped to appreciate the ways in which movement through the water may be achieved. To encourage full involvement and to check on the pupils' understanding, the teacher should ask them questions from time to time.

d) It should be remembered that the development of skill is an individual procedure. This requires a flexible teaching approach and the setting of tasks which the pupils can attempt at their own levels of ability and aptitude.

e) Confidence will be gained through the presentation of carefully graded tasks, related to the needs of the pupils, with adequate time allowed for repetition and consolidation of the skills learned.

f) Careful observation will enable the teacher to assess the requirements of individuals and groups. Then, with appropriate comment and encouragement, pupil performance should be constantly refined and reinforced. Thus an effective working relationship between teacher and pupil can develop.

Artificial Aids

In the early stages the use of artificial aids will be found helpful in assisting the pupils to achieve a floating position and enjoy the thrill of moving through the water. There are various suitable types on the market, the most popular being arm bands, inflatable rings and floats.

The pupils should be allowed to experiment with a variety of aids since different pupils require different types of support. They should then be given one type, or a combination, according to their needs. To avoid possible mishaps the fitting of arm bands or inflatable rings should, however, be carefully supervised before the pupils are allowed to enter the water.

Various methods of entry may be adopted, with the pupils being encouraged to move around the pool, making use of their aids, once they are in the water. At first they should be taught to walk around by sliding their feet along the floor of the pool. It is important to try to keep the shoulders below the water surface, and to ensure that the pupils are not allowed to move out of their depth. Most children, once they have mastered the technique of

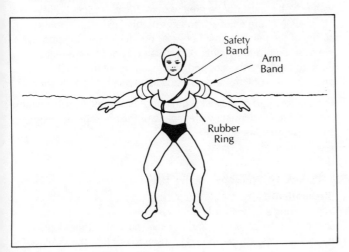

Safety Band

Arm Band

Rubber Ring

Fig. 5·1

walking in water, will enjoy races or competitions involving walking across the pool width.

However, since the main object is to assist the children to be able to take their feet off the bottom of the pool and later to achieve a horizontal position in the water, they should be given the opportunity of experiencing the support that water provides. With shoulders under, and arms spread to assist balance, they should be encouraged to lift the feet and move the arms to produce sideways or turning movement. This practice is sometimes referred to as 'Marking time'.

Later, with shoulders under the water and with arms extended and holding a float, the pupils should attempt to walk forward, taking long steps and raising one leg behind. This should lead some of them to realise that they are in a near prone position and that the use of upward and downward leg actions will assist them to move forward through the water.

Some may find that by holding a supporting float under each arm and walking in a backward direction they will move into supine position. Then, with suitable upward and downward movements of the legs they will experience the thrill of 'swimming' on the back. However, in the early stages of learning to swim, since not all children feel safe in a supine position, it should not be expected that this will prove suitable for every pupil.

Some pupils will enjoy almost immediate success after attempting these practices and should be taught to modify their actions, as a means of improving their ability to move through the water. They may soon be able to discard floats or change from one aid to another before being shown how to make their leg and arm actions more propulsive. Freedom of choice should be allowed, since some of the pupils will take quite naturally to a 'dog paddle' type of arm movement, while others will show a more natural inclination to the simultaneous movements of the arms as performed in the Breast Stroke.

For some pupils, however, the reliance on aids may last for a very long time and this should not be regarded as unusual.

Whatever the approach, it should be the aim of the teacher to help each of the pupils to gain an awareness of the body in water, to develop confidence and to experience the thrill of moving through the water as early as possible in the lessons. Pupils should be encouraged to feel the resistance and the support of the water by pushing and pressing movements with arms, legs and body; to change direction whilst walking; to turn in different ways; to perform jumps; to develop sculling actions with the hands; to float in different body shapes; and to roll from front to back. The task is to encourage and assist by suggesting ways in which the children may improve their performances, with explanations and demonstrations as required. Some may be encouraged to try a different type of aid; others to reduce the buoyancy of inflatable aids by letting out air a little at a time or, to dispense with an aid if sufficiently confident to try without. Although the desirable amount of shallow water may not be available, at least an adequate number of suitable artificial aids can be provided and these should be checked at regular intervals, to ensure that they are fit for use.

Shallow Water Method

In pools where there is water shallow enough for the pupils to support themselves horizontally at the surface, by placing their hands on the bottom of the pool and keeping their heads clear of the water, they may learn through what is known as the Shallow Water Method (fig. 5·2). From this starting position, the pupil should be encouraged to walk through the water using the

hands, with the body extended and the legs trailing behind. When the pupil has experienced the upthrust provided by the water, sufficient confidence should be gained which will allow an attempt to move the legs gently up and down, alternately. If the movements of the hands, in a dog paddle type action are now added, swimming movements will develop. Less confident pupils may still require the support of arm bands or a rubber ring at the start, but these should be dispensed with as soon as the movements have been mastered and confidence has grown.

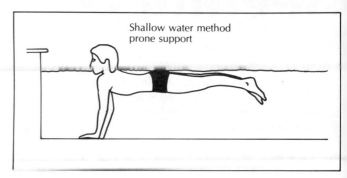

Fig. 5·2

Fig. 5·3

A similar exercise, leading to swimming on the back, is to allow the pupils to sit on the bottom of the pool, supported by the arms. Gentle pressure on the hands will cause the legs to rise towards the surface and a near supine position to be achieved (fig. 5·3). By walking backwards on the hands and then adopting an alternating up and down action with the legs, some pupils will quickly experience the feeling of swimming on the back. If sculling type movements of the hands are used at this stage, the back lying position will be maintained and propulsion through the water will be easier.

It should be emphasised that for the Shallow Water Method, water depths must not be greater than 30cm – 45cm (12in – 18in). One of the chief advantages of this method lies in the ability of the pupil to kneel or sit or on the floor of the pool with the head comfortably clear of the water. Should movement through the water be stopped, the regaining of the position presents no problems and so leads to a feeling of confidence.

The shallow end of the swimming pool is not necessarily suitable unless there is adequate water space of the appropriate depth previously mentioned.

The Early Stages of Teaching

Preparation
In preparing a lesson for beginners, care should be taken to ensure that the physical conditions are suitable. If the depth of the pool varies, a rope should be used to enclose the shallow water area. All aids should be to hand having been previously

checked to see that they are safe. If floats are to be used by the class, they should be arranged around the pool-side. As they assemble on the side of the pool, the children should be prepared for their first lesson by the teacher indicating the water depths and showing the areas of shallow water where they will be working. This information should be repeated and the use of the whistle as a signal to the class to stop, look and listen, should be explained.

At this point, aids such as rings and arm bands should be fitted and then inspected to ensure that they fit snugly. As the sketch shows, the use of a tape will ensure that the ring does not slip down but remains secure.

Entry

Where there are steps provided, it will be found that the children soon grasp the importance of entering by the method shown, i.e. facing the steps and placing the feet carefully on the steps as they descend (fig. 5·4). Some children who are confident may be ready to try one of the other safe methods of entry:

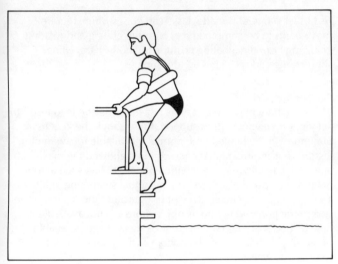

Fig. 5·4

a) Sitting on the poolside, grasping the rail or trough with one hand, the pupil then turns his body sideways, grasping the rail or trough with the other hand and drops into the water. Some pupils may find it easier to enter by using a corner of the pool for this practice.

b) From a standing position, the pupil steps from the poolside to drop into the water towards a competent partner, already in position in the water, to offer support, if required.

c) From a standing position the pupil enters with a jump.

Movement in the water

Pupils should be encouraged to keep on the move immediately after entering the water. Some may need to remain near the poolside with one hand on the rail or trough, the other hand sculling to help maintain balance. All should be encouraged to move about freely with shoulders below the surface of the water to experience its all round support. In addition, should the air temperature be below that of the water there is less chance of feeling chilled if most of the body is kept submerged. As previously mentioned, pupils should practise sliding the feet along the bottom of the pool until they can move about confidently. A float held out in front may be used, sometimes, to help maintain balance or as a stimulus. Later, pupils can be encouraged to vary the length of step, to move in different directions, to change speed and at the same time discover how actions of their arms can affect movement through the water.

Submerging and Breathing Activities

Once pupils are able to move around with confidence in free formation in shallow water, they should be introduced to practices which accustom them to having water on the face, to breathing out, on or under the surface and eventually to submerging. Examples of suitable practices are:

a) Blowing objects along the water surface, e.g. table tennis balls.

b) Immersing the face and blowing out under water for a few seconds.

c) Moving and submerging on a signal from the teacher.

d) Moving over and under the water, using apparatus to encourage submerging, e.g. hoops, weighted rings and tubes.

e) Picking up discs or other objects from the floor of the pool.

f) Touching the pool floor within different parts of the body.

On surfacing, pupils should be encouraged to allow water to run off rather than to wipe their faces.

Getting the Feet off the Bottom of the Pool

Earlier in the chapter one method of getting the feet off the bottom of the pool was explained. Further practices, leading to a horizontal position, are given below:—

a) Walking across the pool with shoulders submerged, chin on the surface and arms forward for support, the pupils lean forward and gradually increase the speed of movement until the feet rise from the bottom of the pool.

b) With shoulders in the water and with arms straight, pupils grasp the rail, raising one leg backwards. Partners standing behind or at the side assist the performers to lie out flat with legs together and just under the surface. In some cases pupils may find it easier to adopt an undergrasp position at the rail and achieve a horizontal position by pressing strongly against the wall of the pool with the forearms.

c) Facing the wall of the pool, a little more than arms' length away, shoulders submerged, arms stretched forward, hands on the surface. From this starting position pupils lean forward and push towards the wall. The movements should be unhurried and smooth, so that the pupils glide towards the rail to grasp it and stand up. As confidence grows, the children should be encouraged to increase the distance they stand away from the wall of the pool. Initially, because of fear, many pupils will be inclined to keep the face out of the water. They should, however, be asked to take a breath and to place the face in the water before pushing in towards the wall, in order to achieve a more streamlined position.

d) Working in pairs, with one pushing from the wall and gliding to a partner who, standing ready to assist at a short distance away, helps him to regain his feet. The supporter moves further away, as the performer gains in confidence, and provides gradually decreasing support until the performer is happy to push away from the wall and glide in a horizontal extended position, unaided. Pupils should be encouraged to stretch out gradually and smoothly, after a firm and deliberate push from the wall of the pool. Sudden or jerky movements should be avoided. This practice may be performed in prone or supine positions.

Regaining the Standing Position

Once a pupil can assume a horizontal position in the water and is able to propel himself along, it is an appropriate time to teach, as a safety measure, the ways in which the pupil can regain the standing position. If the pupil is in the extended prone position, all that is required is for the knees to be tucked, downward

Fig 5·5 Regaining Standing position

pressure to be applied with the hands, and the head lifted. The feet can then be pushed downwards and placed firmly on the bottom of the pool (fig. 5·5). To regain the standing position from the back lying position the arms make a preparatory downward-backward press. They continue to move forward and upward with a circling action, similar to the movement in skipping backward. At the same time the head is raised forward and the knees are raised towards the chest. The resulting reactions cause the body to rotate to a vertical position from which standing position can be regained with the arms outspread to assist balance (fig. 5·6). In both instances the shoulders should be kept in the water throughout the movements. Practices with partners may be found useful. In the prone position, the pupil faces a supporter, who holds his outstretched hands. The performer should then attempt the three movements of pressing the arms downwards, tucking and lifting the head to stand up. If support is required, assistance can be given at any time during the practice. Similarly, with the pupil lying in an extended position on the back, the supporter can stand behind with hands under the shoulders and if required, gentle pressure can be applied to help him stand up. It is recommended that this method of regaining the standing position is known before a back stroke is taught.

Once pupils are able to push and glide on the front and on the back and to regain a standing position they should be given practices to enable them to rotate from a prone to a supine position and vice versa. Initially, these should take place in shallow water until pupils develop confidence in their ability to rotate, simply by tilting the body in the desired direction and using the hands and arms to assist the movement.

As pupils become increasingly aware of the support which water offers, they should be encouraged to explore different ways of floating on the front and on the back with the body assuming different shapes – long, wide, curled, etc.

As further progress is made, tasks can be set which require movements to be combined e.g. pushing, gliding and rotating; changing from one floating position to another; travelling submerging and springing up to resurface.

Partner Support
Although there may be occasions when it is desirable to resort to activities involving partner support, these should be kept to a minimum. In the limited time normally available for swimming lessons, it is important that each child be allowed the maximum amount of activity. Working with a partner reduces the amount of time each pupil is involved in the actual swimming practices and this is not an efficient way of using water time. However, in swimming pools where floats or handrails are not available it may be necessary for partners to give support, e.g. to enable pupils to get their feet off the bottom of the pool or to be towed through the water.

Timid Pupils
Special attention is required in cases of extreme timidity, where a pupil simply will not enter the water, even when ample swimming aids are provided or shallow water is available.

The teacher should adopt a patient and sympathetic attitude and never attempt to force the pace. It is sometimes helpful to allow

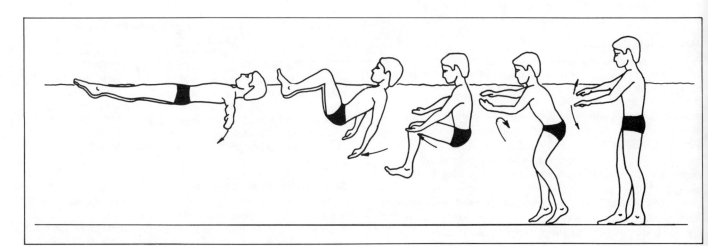

Fig 5·6 Regaining Standing position

a nervous pupil to watch the others in the class enjoying themselves in the water and thus feel motivated to join in with them. From a sitting position by the steps at the edge of the pool the pupil can be encouraged to try to find a way gradually, down into the water.

If it can be arranged to have an assistant nearby, so much the better. With a gentle and encouraging approach even the most timid of children is likely to respond, unless there is some serious psychological block. If the pool temperature is at a comfortable level, the chances of entry, through persuasion, will be enhanced. The support of artificial aids will also be found to be an important factor in achieving success with a reluctant or nervous pupil. It should be said, also, that lessons of short duration will be found more suitable. Indeed, a teacher who is sensitive to pupil needs and aware of any fears will probably achieve more by responding to a request to participate only for a part of the lesson than the teacher who insists on the pupil remaining in or at the side of the pool for the entire duration of the lesson, shivering and miserable. Knowing that they can go and get dried and dressed when they feel they have had enough, timid pupils will more likely want to take part in subsequent lessons and will not feel deterred by the teacher's disapproving attitude as well as their own fears.

Once a nervous pupil can be enticed to enter the water, steps should be taken to direct attention outwards. This can be accomplished by providing a ball, quoit or similar object to play with. If the children are allowed to pass the ball or quoit to one another, they are less likely to concern themselves with inner feelings and will probably enjoy the experience of simple game-like activities of short duration. Since most nervous children are upset by water which is rough or by splashing, they should be allowed to use a quiet section of shallow water wherever possible.

Over a period of time, when the initial fear of entering and moving in the water has been overcome, it should be possible to introduce timid pupils to some of the activities mentioned at the beginning of the chapter, e.g. holding on to the rail or trough and pulling themselves along, walking races, etc. Progress will most likely be slow, but this is of secondary importance to the building of confidence and the realisation that swimming is enjoyable. With really difficult cases, however, where a pupil does not respond to such methods as these, should be given individual attention and taught as a handicapped person.

Young Children

Parent and Baby Classes
In appropriate conditions babies may learn to swim even before they can walk. Certainly, the introduction of babies to a total environment of water, not merely the water in the bath at home (see below), is accepted with no more apprehension than any new situation to which they may be subjected outside the familiar home surroundings.

Evidence of this is seen in the increasing number of Parent/Baby classes during the last few years. However, for success in such enterprises, certain requirements are recommended over and above those which are usual in learning to swim classes.

These are as follows:

a) Water space preferably shallow overall, with a temperature of 28°–30°C (82°–86°F). Off-peak swimming times are obviously the best.

b) For comfort, an air temperature approaching 1° above that of the water.

c) A warm changing room.

d) Suitable mats on which babies may be changed.

e) Chairs for the use of parents while changing babies.

f) A container for soiled napkins.

g) Cribs or playpen in which babies can be placed while parents are changing.

h) A wide range of swimming aids and suitable toys at the pool side, for the teacher and parents to select, as required.

i) Resuscitation equipment suitable for young babies, immediately available.

The appointment of the right teachers for this specialist job is very important. It is sometimes considered an advantage if they have children of their own for this may help in relationships with other parents. The teachers must be qualified to teach swimming and some medical knowledge is an advantage. Certainly, competence in the use of resuscitation equipment is necessary. Before organising such classes for the first time, it is advisable to consult with someone who has had previous practical experience.

Lessons

At Home
Early experience in preparation for visits to the large pool may be given in the bath at home. Water should be approximately 33°C (91°F). With baby in the supine position and supported under the back of the head and seat, movements of the arms and legs can be encouraged. Moving baby backwards and forwards can create waves. Baby can be lifted from oncoming water but some water from the opposite direction may be allowed to wash over the head and face.

At the Pool
It is considered that 10 parents with their babies is the maximum number with which one teacher can cope, for safety, and to instruct adequately.

At first, regular time tables may be found difficult to arrange until parents have adjusted their routines to the required time of day for classes. Thereafter, regularity of attendance should be encouraged in order to keep the classes balanced. The pool-side should be made as homely as possible with sounds and objects familiar to small babies. A variety of toys, similar to those used in the bath at home, will encourage movement once the babies are in the water.

If there is a wide age range, possibly 3 months to 3 years, a formal lesson cannot be carried out. Parents are advised, individually, how best to keep babies happy in the water. The aim is to accustom them to the water, to provide situations in which confidence can be gained and the support of the water enjoyed.

Having left the changing area the parent takes the baby to the teacher at the pool-side. At this stage appropriate aids are fitted. It is considered dangerous for the parent to enter the water whilst carrying the baby. The baby is held by the teacher and handed to the parent in the water. The reverse procedure is followed when the parent wishes to leave the water.

Much later, when the child is capable of sitting on the pool-side, always with supervision, the parent may enter, then lift the child into the water or encourage a jump. Where there are steps, the parent, in the water, can provide support for the child to climb in, always facing the wall.

The following are some of the activities which have been found successful:

a) The parent holds the baby in an upright position, close to the body, with faces at the same level, then sinks in the water, unhurriedly, while assessing the baby's reactions.

b) Still holding the baby, the parent blows bubbles for the baby to see and to feel.

c) With feet firmly on the pool bottom the parent 'bobs' up and down.

d) Many young babies can float unaided on their backs, if relaxed and not concerned with water on the face. The parent supports from a sideways-on position with one hand under the head and one hand under the seat. The parent should be positioned in the water with the face level with the baby. Provided that the parent is feeling confident and the baby is relaxed, support may be gradually reduced.

e) Supporting as in d), the baby can be moved backwards and forwards.

f) When the baby begins to sit up, the same position tends to be adopted in the water. Support may now be given under the chin and under the tummy and forward and backward movements may be made with baby in the prone position.

g) When the head can be self supported, baby can be held in front of the parent with support under the armpits, with or without arm bands, and towing movements may be made. Baby's natural movements of the arms and legs can be encouraged and, as confidence in floating develops, support may be carefully reduced. Towards the end of this type of activity, baby can be happily moving around in an upright position, similar to treading water. If a favourite toy is placed in front, this will encourage baby to move towards it. The parent will be ever watchful and ready to provide support and reassurance, whether or not buoyancy aids are used.

h) By encouraging pulling and kicking movements, and the adoption of a more horizontal position, resulting from towing, support may be transferred to the lower arms. Occasionally, the arms may be directed into a 'dog-paddle' type of movement or similarly, the legs may be supported and gently moved up and down.

i) As the child begins to move in the water unaided, attention should be focussed on further confidence-building practices and exploring different ways of moving, rather than attempting to copy the strokes of other children. At this stage, no attempts should be made to teach formal stroke movements.

If arm bands are found to be cumbersome, the amount of air may be reduced or double arm bands can be halved to provide just a single chamber, which allows for greater freedom.

References to age have been omitted, because progress will be related to the age at which babies are first introduced to the water and to their general development which can vary so much. All sessions should be enjoyable, unhurried and suited to the babies' needs.

Adult Learners

As many adults have never learned to swim, either through lack of opportunity or through various difficulties when young, the provision of classes for adults is desirable. In fact, many authorities now provide instructional classes for adults only, and it is pleasing to note that these are increasing in popularity.

Those who join such classes are usually highly motivated and need little stimulus from the teacher. This helps to compensate for lack of natural ability or in general flexibility that becomes apparent with age.

Classes which have proved most successful are those which are arranged at times when the general public are excluded from the pool and when there are no children present. This arrangement helps to avoid any embarrassment which some adult learners experience when they find difficulty in carrying out the water practices.

The teacher must consider carefully the wide age range of participants which is quite likely. It is important also to be aware of any physical disabilities which may affect the learning rate and which may require adaption of orthodox swimming strokes. Adult learners may lack strength and/or flexibility and they may have difficulty in hearing or seeing the teacher.

Often they will not have participated in any form of exercise for many years and the translation of words into appropriate actions may prove difficult. Instructions should be stated in simple language, avoiding jargon and emphasis should be upon fundamentals of movement in water rather than special stroke techniques. It is often helpful to give reasons for certain actions to be performed, in addition to merely outlining them.

In the early stages, an experienced swimmer acting as a helper in the water can assist the teacher by demonstrating the various practices and, later, show individuals how to perform the actions.

Just as young children benefit from the use of artificial aids, so too will adult learners. The teacher's approach must be modified to suit the older pupils, and patience, good humour and encouragement will achieve wonders.

The aims should be the same, in general terms, as those applying to classes of children. The ability to get the feet off the bottom of the pool, to achieve a comfortable position either on the back or the front and to experience the feeling of propulsion through the water, resulting from appropriate limb movements, should be the initial aim. Later, through the use of a Multi-Stroke approach the class should be introduced to the main strokes and allowed to choose the stroke which gives them most success as individuals.

Should one be faced with a nervous adult in the special Adult Learner class, much of what applies to the treatment of the timid child will apply here. However, if it can be arranged for a capable and willing helper to enter the water to give support and confidence, then this has advantages.

In recognising the need to provide incentives, the ASA has introduced a series of Adult Proficiency Awards, details of which may be obtained from the ASA Office.

Chapter 6

Breast Stroke

Breast Stroke is the oldest of the four modern competitive strokes and is used widely by swimmers of all abilities. It is often taught as a first stroke because the swimmer is in a prone position which allows him to look forward. Furthermore the need for aquatic breathing can be avoided by keeping the mouth above the water throughout the stroke.

These advantages combine to promote confidence in the beginner. The stroke has mechanical disadvantages which make it the slowest of the competitive strokes. This is because the recovery of the legs and arms beneath the surface of the water creates considerable resistance when swimming at speed; the propulsive efforts are less continuous than those of the crawl strokes; the relatively high position of the head, especially when inhaling, causes the body to be inclined from the horizontal, producing additional resistance.

Therefore, it is important to try to achieve the best possible combination of minimum resistance and maximum propulsion from well co-ordinated and mechanically efficient movements. Unlike the other competitive strokes, Breast Stroke derives great propulsive effect from the leg action, due to the strong backward force exerted against the water.

Body Position
The body should be as horizontal as possible (fig. 6·1) whilst allowing the leg action to take place under the surface of the water. This will produce a position which is inclined slightly downwards from the head to the feet. Good streamlining should always be the aim. The underwater recovery movements of the arms and legs, also the lifting of the head to breathe, all greatly interfere with the ideal body position. In order to reduce resistance created by the recovery movements, the legs should remain in a trailing and streamlined position (fig. 6·2) as the arm pull takes place. Similarly, when the powerful leg kick is propelling the body forward the arms should be fully extended and frontal resistance further reduced by lowering the head and keeping it steady and as low as possible (fig. 6·3).

Fig. 6·2

Fig. 6·3

Leg Action
There are two types of leg action:

a) A narrow, 'whip-like' action used by most competitive swimmers and quite naturally adopted by some beginners.

b) A wide, wedge-type action used mainly by recreational swimmers and some beginners.

Whip Kick
Recovery. From the extended position the heels are drawn up towards the seat and are about hip width apart. The position of the knees may vary from being fairly close together to a position just outside the body width. The angle between the upper leg and trunk when viewed from the side varies from 110° to 140°. If the angle is greater than this the propulsive effect is reduced and if it is less, resistance is increased. At this stage the lower legs are in a near perpendicular position with the feet turned outward and the soles of the feet facing uppermost and just below the water surface (figs. 6·4, 6·5).

Fig. 6·1

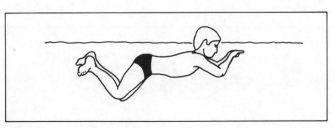

Fig. 6·4

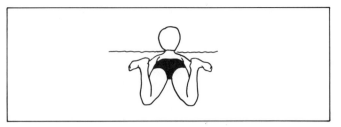

Fig. 6·5

Propulsion. The feet are driven mainly backward, following a curved pathway as they move towards each other. This is a smooth, powerful and accelerating movement. The drive is first made with the inner sides of the feet and lower legs, using a whip-like action as they thrust vigorously against the water. Then the broad paddles of the feet fix on the water, enabling the body to be driven forward as the legs are extended. (figs. 6·6, 6·7).

Fig. 6·6

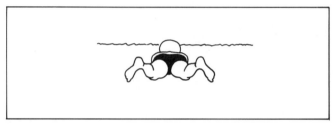

Fig. 6·7

Wedge Kick

The wedge kick has a slower tempo than the whip kick. Consequently, it gives a more relaxed stroke. It is the type of action adopted by many recreative swimmers and it is often used with beginners.

Recovery. From the extended position the feet are drawn upwards toward the seat. In so doing the knees will move forward-outward with the heels held almost together (figs. 6·8, 6·9). The whole movement should be performed without any tension.

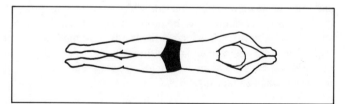

Fig. 6·8

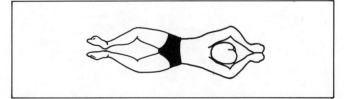

Fig. 6·9

Propulsion. From this position of recovery the feet drive outwards and backwards, the toes being turned towards the shin so that the soles of the feet face backwards, the heels lead the legs in an outward and inward sweep until they come together with the ankles touching.

The movement gains impetus as the feet and legs move backwards, pushing against the water (figs. 6·10, 6·11).

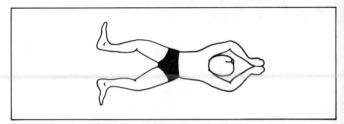

Fig. 6·10

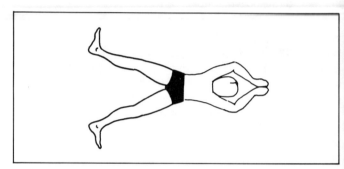

Fig. 6·11

Arm Action

The natural stroke has a continuous circling action without any pause or glide. However, the stroke is improved when a short glide is used. The speed swimmer reduces the glide to a minimum, but it is still important that the hands pass through the glide position even if a pause in the action is not apparent. The arm action has two main variations;

a) a bent arm pull with a high elbow used by most competitive swimmers,

b) a straight arm pull suitable for the beginner and recreative swimmer.

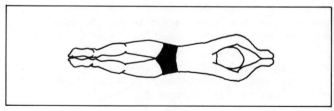

Fig. 6·12

Fig. 6·13

Bent Arm Pull

Propulsion. The propulsive phase begins with the arms in a fully extended position, the hands being close together at a depth of 15 to 20cm (6in – 8in) (fig. 6·12). The hands turn slightly outward and begin to pull in an outward and downward direction until they reach a position in front of and slightly outside the width of the shoulders (fig. 6·13).

Fig. 6·14

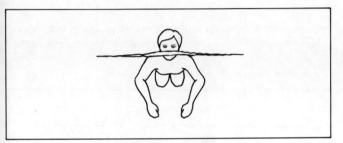

Fig. 6·15

Pressure is now sharply increased and continues to increase throughout the remainder of the propulsive phase. At this stage the elbows start to bend and at the same time, the hands turn so that the palms face towards the feet and the fingers point towards the bottom of the pool (fig. 6·14).

The hands start to pull backwards and the elbows continue to bend but remain in a high position. With the hands beneath the elbows and before they reach the shoulder line they begin to move inwards to finish the propulsive action (fig. 6·15).

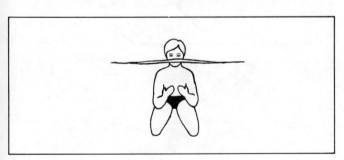

Fig. 6·16

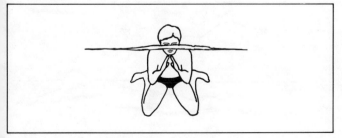

Fig. 6·17

Recovery. The arms should move quickly into the recovery by releasing their purchase on the water with a swirling action. The arms are brought close together within the body width, the position of the palms at this point varying from facing upwards to downwards (figs. 6·16, 6·17). The recovery is completed as the arms are moved smoothly forward at or under the surface of the water to return to the starting position (fig. 6·18).

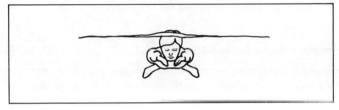

Fig. 6·18

Straight Arm Pull

Propulsion. From the extended position the palms turn outwards and the arms pull downward—outward and backwards. This action continues until the arms have reached a position in front of, and slightly outside, the shoulder line (making an angle between themselves of approximately 90°) (fig. 6·19).

The finger tips will be about 30cm (12in) below the surface of the water. At this stage the arms are almost straight and the swimmer should be able to see the hands without turning the head.

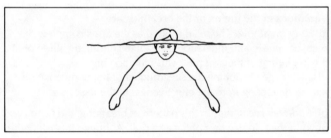

Fig. 6·19

Recovery. As the hands and arms reach this position, the elbows bend and drop with the hands moving together, the palms facing downwards. The elbows are kept well into the sides during this part of the movement, for effective streamlining (fig. 6·20). From this position the arms are extended smoothly forward to the starting position (fig. 6·21).

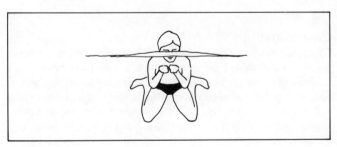

Fig. 6·20

Fig. 6·21

Breathing

There is wide choice in the technique of breathing in this stroke. Although this may not be of any great consequence to the average performer, the position of the head during breathing can influence the stroke considerably.

Some swimmers keep the head raised throughout the full stroke cycle so that the mouth and nose can be clear of the water surface at all times, simplifying the breathing.

This style will certainly cause the hips to drop and will increase frontal resistance considerably.

A better position is that in which the head is held still, with the water level between the bridge of the nose and the hair line. However, the head must be raised to breathe, and if assisted by the downward pressure of the arms, an unwanted loss of horizontal poise will result, leading to increased frontal resistance.

The best compromise between the necessity to breathe and the mechanical disadvantages that ensue, is achieved by smoothly lifting the head by the minimum amount. Inhalation should take place through the mouth with the head being returned to the normal position before the leg drive begins. This is achieved by pushing the chin forward, sufficient only for the mouth to clear the water. Exhalation takes place through the mouth and nose, preferably when the face is immersed.

Variations in the timing of the breathing are:–

a) *Early breathing.* The head is lifted as the arms complete the recovery phase and inhalation takes place during the glide or at the beginning of the arm pull. This variation has the disadvantage of spoiling the streamlining of the body position and so detracting from the effectiveness of the leg drive.

b) *Mid-way breathing.* In this pattern of breathing, the head is lifted in the midway part of the arm pull. Although this is not the most efficient technique it is the one most often used by beginners and recreative swimmers.

c) *Late breathing.* This is the one invariably used by competitive swimmers, inhalation taking place between the end of the propulsive phase and the start of the recovery phase. It is important that any pause, which might occur when breathing is taking place, is reduced to a minimum.

Co-ordination

The co-ordination of the propulsive actions of the arms and legs is one of continuous alternation, so that, as one propulsive movement ceases, the other takes over. The stroke sequence is basically, pull-breathe-kick-glide. The length of the glide in the sprint is minimal. The legs are fully extended when the arm pull begins, but before it is completed, the legs begin to recover. As the arms recover, the legs continue with their recovery and as the arms move towards full extension, the leg kick should have just begun.

Variations. Many variations in Breast Stroke are to be seen. These are dependent on individual strength, mobility and length of limb. For example, some swimmers with strong upper extremities gain a greater degree of propulsion from the arm pull while others derive greater propulsion from their legs. Variations in rhythm may also be found. Competitive swimmers in sprint events may use an almost 'continuous' stroke in which alternate arm and leg actions can be co-ordinated, to give a more effective propulsion. This is achieved by allowing the beginning of the arm pull to coincide with the completion of the backward thrust of the legs and by starting the recovery of the legs, as the arms are completing their propulsive phase.

Teaching the Stroke

Children learn by regularly practising activities appropriate to their levels of ability. In the early stages, with the help of a ring, arm bands or similar aids, the simultaneous circling movements of the arms can be achieved quickly and with a reasonable degree of success. In the first stages of stroke performance, the body may be held in an almost vertical position, because of the desire to keep the face and mouth well clear of the water. However, as confidence develops, the learner will be prepared to lower the head, to adopt a more horizontal position in the water. In the first exploratory stages the emphasis will have been on the arm action, but it will soon become apparent that the leg kick must receive attention.

Because of its importance in the stroke, leg practices will require to feature prominently in the early lessons. However, in keeping

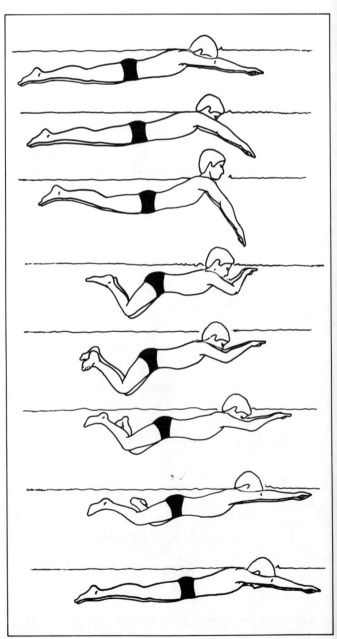

Breast Stroke Sequence

42

with the whole-part-whole approach, described elsewhere in this book, immediately following any successful leg practices, there should be attempts at swimming the whole stroke. At this stage, it is important to stress the correct performance of the leg action, otherwise faults will develop which might become permanent. Breathing and timing seldom present difficulties after a good leg action has been established. However, 'aquatic breathing' must be learned before a swimmer is able to adopt a flatter position in the water and for good style to develop.

Teaching Practices and Teaching Points
Body position

a) Attempts at swimming the full stroke with the aid of a buoyancy aid at the waist.

b) Push and glide practices with or without a buoyancy aid.

c) Full stroke swimming, holding the breath and with the head in the correct position. This practice can be used with or without aids.

d) Full stroke swimming and introducing the breathing action.

Teaching points
Keep the head steady; Keep the shoulders level; Look directly forward at a spot just below the surface (the depth of this spot will vary according to the natural buoyancy of the swimmer); Keep the hips high in the water.

Leg action
The main aim in the initial stages is to establish a basic symmetrical kick with flat feet. Some swimmers will acquire the 'whip' action easily, while others will have more success with the 'wedge' kick. Teachers should, therefore, be prepared to accept either version.

In the first instance a learner should attempt the whole stroke, with buoyancy aids if necessary. This gives the opportunity to see any faults in the leg kick. If the flat-footed kick is natural to the learner, a period of consolidation will be needed with helpful suggestions such as 'kick back harder.' If, however as is often the case with the learner, there is difficulty in controlling the feet, it may be necessary to return to first principles.

Teaching practices
a) *Out of water.* Show the difference between flat feet and pointed toes. Show how to direct the feet outwards, i.e. 'turn the feet east and west.'

b) *In the water.* Grasping the rail. (It will help if the learner has a buoyancy aid round the hips).

i) Adopt an extended position with feet turned outward.

ii) Keeping the feet in this position, practise the full action using either 'whip' or 'wedge' kick.

c) If the complete movement is unsatisfactory, it will be necessary to break down the practice into two parts, i.e. first bending the knees and obtaining the correct position, then completing the kick.

d) In exceptional cases, it may be necessary to have a competent helper directing the movement of the heels. As soon as the correct action is achieved, the swimmer should try the full stroke again.

e) Once the correct kick has been mastered, practice kicking and gliding. (One or more kicks).

f) Try swimming the width of the pool using the fewest possible kicks. (Using a float in the early stages).

g) Full stroke practices, holding the glide to encourage more power from the leg kick.

Teaching points
Emphasise that the feet drive mainly backward with the heels leading; keep the toes pointed during recovery and at the end of the drive; after recovery turn the feet outward.

Arm action
Most swimmers have little difficulty in learning some form of Breast Stroke arm movement. The beginner will understand simple suggestions such as 'move the hands in circles.' It may be necessary with a difficult pupil to practise the arm movement while standing in shallow water, with one foot forward and with the shoulders below the surface.

The main problem in the early stage is to prevent the hands pulling past the shoulders. It helps to suggest 'try to see your hands in front of you all the time.'

Teaching practices
a) Push and glide followed by complete arm action and leg kick. Try to get a good glide.

b) Increase the number of stroke cycles, concentrating on the correct performance of the arm action.

Teaching points
Keep the arms extended and close together at the start of the pull; Keep the elbows close to the sides during recovery; Extend the arms forward, smoothly and quickly, following the arm pull.

Breathing
In the initial stages little difficulty should be encountered because the face will be out of the water.

Most beginners will breathe naturally as the arms pull because this tends to raise the upper part of the body. They should be encouraged to push the chin forward to breathe without lifting the shoulders. At a later stage, the swimmer will learn to breathe as the pull finishes. It is the role of a good teacher to decide whether or not to introduce later breathing. Greater success may be achieved by allowing the swimmer to retain the breathing pattern which was first used.

Co-ordination
If all the preceding practices have been regularly and well performed, the combining of the arms and legs and breathing should present little difficulty.

Teaching practices
a) Use pushing and gliding practices followed by pulling and breathing and kicking.

b) Indicate the sequence and rhythm using the words – pull, breathe, kick, glide.

c) In the early stages it may be helpful to prolong the glide to establish an unhurried stroke.

Faults	Causes	Corrections
1) Uneven or 'screw kick'.	a) Turning the head to the side to facilitate breathing. b) Turning one foot in a different manner from the other (e.g. one foot extended and one dorsi-flexed). c) One knee higher than the other.	a) Breathing practices; keep the head steady and shoulders square to water. b) Return to early practices described under 'Leg action'. (Usually it will be necessary to draw attention to the incorrect foot). c) Kick with a small float gripped in between upper legs or kick with knees touching. d) Practise on the back, concentrating on a more symmetrical leg action, and check it.
2) Uneven arm pull. (e.g. pulling too deeply with one arm and too wide with the other).	a) A weak leg action makes the arms do all the work. b) Fear, causing the head to turn for breathing. c) Mistaken idea that it gives greater propulsion.	a) It may be necessary to re-teach the leg action. Encourage kick-glide. b) Encourage breath holding to establish a good head position in the water. Learn aquatic breathing. c) Re-teach arm action.
3) Pulling too far back.	a) As for (c) above.	a) As for (c) above. Emphasise that the arm action takes place in front of the shoulders.
4) Bobbing too high in the water.	a) Bringing knees too far under the body. b) Incorrect timing. c) Lifting the head too high to breathe.	a) Practise with float between upper legs. Encourage heels to the surface on recovery. b) Encourage pull, breathe, kick. Insist on glide after the kick. c) Keep the head steady. Suggest that chin is on the water when breath is taken. Keep shoulders steady.

Reader's notes

Reader's notes

Chapter 7

Back Crawl

At the beginning of the century two forms of back stroke were being performed. Both had leg actions similar in shape and pathway to that of a wide inverted Breast Stroke but the arm actions differed. In the Elementary Back Stroke the arms were moved, simultaneously, from shoulder level to the sides of the body, followed by an underwater recovery. The English Back Stroke was faster, by reason of a longer arm pull from beyond the head, and an out of water recovery. The continuing quest for speed, brought about an alternating arm action and later, an alternating upward and downward leg kick leading to the development of the Back Crawl Stroke. The modern version of the stroke has the arm action balanced by the leg kick, accompanied by a noticeable body roll and reaction at the hips and feet. The degree of reaction depends upon the performer's physical characteristics, associated with the application of basic techniques.

The earlier strokes are still performed for various reasons and fuller descriptions appear in the chapter on Recreative Swimming.

Body Position
The body is as horizontal as possible consistent with the performance of an effective leg action taking place completely under, but near the water surface. The back of the head is in the water with the hips high. The knees remain below the surface and the toes just dimple the surface on the up kick (fig. 7·1).

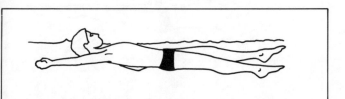

Fig. 7·1

The position of the head is important because a raised head makes a 'hips-up' position difficult, leading to a type of sitting position in the water. Since poor floaters find it difficult to achieve a comfortable head position, the good teacher should be aware of this when choosing practices and when commenting on body position. A further requirement is that the body is stretched with legs and feet extended and this depends on flexibility and mobility. Swimmers with stiff ankles find the body position and the leg kick difficult to achieve, while others with good flexibility in legs and ankles will adopt a good position naturally. Competent swimmers use a 'shallow dish' shape which places the shoulder girdle and hips in an advantageous position for the effective use of arms and legs.

Leg Action
Efficient Back Crawl swimming depends on an effective leg kick. It is often described as an alternating up and down kick, suggesting an action in a vertical plane. This might well happen when the swimmer is involved in practices with legs only, however, when the arm action is used, the kick is part sideways, part vertical and then partly to the other side.

Before each kick up to the surface the knee bends, due to pressure of the water against the front of the leg and ankle. It is accompanied by some hip extension and movement of the leg backward, relative to the spine (fig. 7·2). With the leg at its lowest position the up kick is initiated by the powerful muscles of the hip. Then the action passes to the muscles which straighten the knee, accelerating the movement of the pointed foot to the surface (fig. 7·3). At this time, intoeing often takes place as a consequence of the natural structure of a flexible ankle joint. Full extension of the knee occurs and the action ends in a whip-like movement of the foot. The toes touch the surface if the pace is easy but there is a lot of broken water in hard paced swimming. The leg remains straight for most of the downward movement with the sole of the foot pressing on the water.

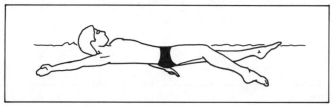

Fig. 7·2

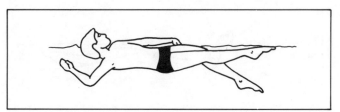

Fig. 7·3

Whether propulsion is obtained depends on the size of feet, ankle mobility and strength of legs. As one leg finishes its upward action the other leg is at its lowest position with the foot some 30-60 cms (12-24ins) below the surface. The feet pass close to each other as the legs move upward and downward.

Arm Action

In Back Crawl it is convenient to think of two possible extremes of action.

a) Bent Arm Action or 'S' pull.

b) Straight Arm Action.

The bent arm technique is the more effective because it uses a shorter lever permitting a faster action and it has a more effective propulsive force, being closer to the line of progression. The straight arm technique is not truly straight because the hand follows a semi-circular pathway, centred on the shoulder, and it is at its deepest opposite the shoulder (fig. 7·4). It will be recalled that a long lever moves more slowly than a short one. It will be recalled, also, that every action produces an equal and opposite reaction and therefore only in the middle part of the straight arm action will there be a fully effective reaction. The first and last thirds of the semicircular action will produce reactions to one side or the other. Observation reveals the straight arm action to be deep, relative to the line across the shoulders. Such action is weak in consideration of the effective use of the strong muscles of shoulder, chest and back (fig. 7·5). This is because the straight arm technique is accompanied by a flatter body position with less roll. For three reasons, therefore, the straight arm technique is less effective than the bent arm one.

a) A long lever moves more slowly giving a slower stroking rate.

b) Mechanically it produces less propulsion.

c) Anatomically it tends to place the muscles of the shoulder joint in a weak position for effective action. If there is elbow bend the elbow tends to lead the hand.

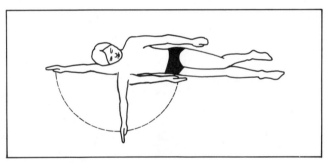

Fig. 7·4

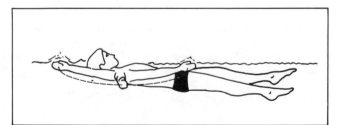

Fig. 7·5

Entry

The entry of the hand is similar for both techniques. It is preferable if the little finger enters in advance of the hand and this requires some rotation of the wrist. If the shoulders are not flexible, the back of the hand enters first and when this happens the hand has to turn as it sinks into the water. Generally, the entry is in line with or very slightly wide of the shoulders but skilled performers tend to move nearer the centre line. (fig. 7·6).

Fig. 7·6

Propulsion

a) Bent Arm Action

Catch. The hand turns and shapes early and in skilled performances there is a distinct press down before purchase is gained at approximately 15 cms (6 ins) (fig. 7·7).

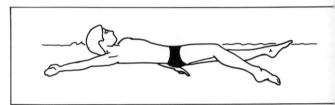

Fig. 7·7

Pull. As the arm pulls, the elbow begins to bend and as the movement continues the arm rotates so that the hand catches up the elbow. The degree of bend, approximately 90°, can vary between individuals and sometimes between right and left arms. The head remains in line with the body, whilst the shoulder on the pulling side drops to obtain the most advantageous position for a strong pull-push action already mentioned (figs. 7·8).

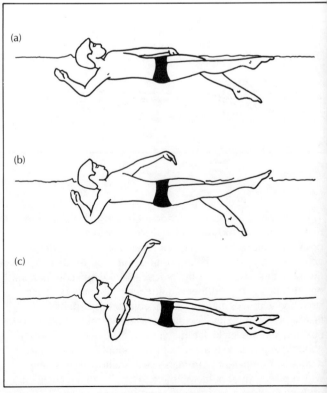

(a)

(b)

(c)

Fig. 7·8

Push. Once the shoulder, elbow and hand are level, they are well positioned for a powerful push. The hand continues to face towards the feet until the arm is fully extended. For many swimmers, especially learners, lack of strength may result in the push being weak in all or in part. If the push is complete, it finishes with a fully extended arm below the hips, the palm of the hand facing the bottom of the pool (figs. 7·9).

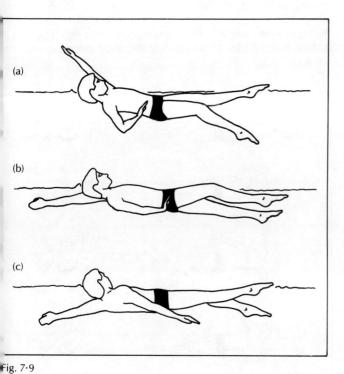

Fig. 7·9

A side view through the whole action shows the hand tracing a pathway rather like a letter 'S' on its side (fig 7·10).

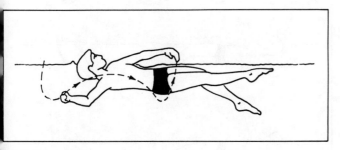

Fig. 7·10

b) Straight Arm Action
In this action the hand follows a semi-circular pathway. After the 'Catch' much of the pull is outward, as the arm increases in depth, until it reaches shoulder level and it is here that propulsion is most effective. As there is very little bending at the elbow, the remainder of the action, the push phase, tends to be inward towards the hip where it finishes. At no time should the hand be lower than body depth. Teachers should note that for many swimmers, the straight arm action is quite comfortable and effective. It is perfectly acceptable, and may be compared with the recreational versions of Breast Stroke, which also use long, nearly straight, arm actions (figs. 7·4 and 7·5).

Recovery
In this phase of the stroke the straight arm is lifted from the water, vertically, and returned directly to the entry position (figs. 7·11). There will be variations of the hand position in recovery and in the manner of arm rotation required to allow the little finger to lead for entry. However, the whole action should allow a smooth and flowing transition between propulsion and re-entry. The rolling of the body aids recovery by raising the upper shoulder clear of the water, thereby reducing resistance.

The re-entry of one arm coincides with the full extension of the other at the end of its propulsive phase.

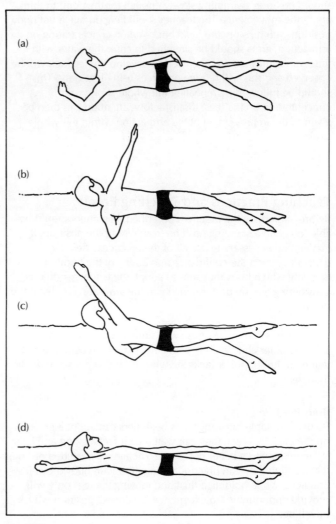

Fig. 7·11

Breathing
As the face is out of the water throughout the stroke, with the body in the supine position, there should be no major breathing problems. Indeed, most swimmers are neither aware of the manner in which they breathe nor at which point in the stroke the breath is taken. They should, however, be encouraged to breathe at regular intervals. This applies particularly to beginners who tend to hold the breath.

Co-ordination

The co-ordination of arm and leg actions develops with practice. Normally, six beats of the legs occur during one complete arm cycle. The opposite leg kicks downward at the beginning of each arm pull. This helps to balance the body as in walking and running, when one arm swings forward as the opposite foot steps forward, and vice versa.

Teaching the Stroke

Back Crawl is probably the easiest stroke to teach. There should be no breathing problems, as in Front Crawl, which has the face in the water. The upward and downward leg action is less complicated than that in Breast Stroke.

Following a good demonstration with comments, the pupil should be allowed to attempt the full stroke. Non-swimmers wearing artificial aids may also try. The emphasis at this stage should be upon swimming slowly enough for the pupil to think about the movements. The teacher should encourage a flat body position with hips up and head back. When concentrating on the arm action, arms should be stretched to enter the water with little or no splash. Soon, the need to develop the leg kick will be observed and this will require practices using legs only. This should be followed by repeating the whole stroke with concentration on the legs. If satisfactory, attention can then be given to the improvement of the arm action within the whole stroke.

Teaching Practices and Teaching Points

Before attempting the practices described, beginners should be able to regain a standing position from the supine position. It may not be necessary to use all of the practices, their use depending upon the confidence and ability of the pupil. In deciding which buoyancy aids to adopt, the teacher should be considering a body position in which the arms are initially at the sides.

Partner support may be of use with adult learners and with selected older children but, generally, maximum benefit is not gained if the supporter lacks knowledge, skill and a sympathetic attitude.

Body Position

By using suitable buoyancy aids beginners can adopt a position on the back in which they can watch their feet kicking and later, stretching out to a better position. To achieve a stretched or 'long leg' position they can practise at the rail or with buoyancy aids. Practices, while holding a float and moving the legs only will provide opportunities to experience the correct position whilst travelling.

Points to emphasize are:
Head back to look upwards: hips up.

Leg Action

The kick may be practised in any of the following ways depending upon the standard already achieved by the pupil:

a) With a float under each arm providing sufficient buoyancy to keep the head comfortably clear of the water.

b) With a float held to support the head.

c) With one or two floats held on the stomach.

d) With one float, held at arms' length, over the thighs or knees.

e) With hands sculling at the sides of the body.

f) Without the use of arms (e.g. hands held by the sides, resting on thighs etc).

g) With arms extended beyond the head. This is an advanced practice and care should be taken to ensure that the swimmer is able to achieve and maintain this position.

In extreme cases of difficulty the teacher may have to guide the legs whilst the pupil is out of the water, or have the assistance of an able pupil in the water.

Points to emphasize are: kick from the hips; long legs; loose ankles; pointed toes; kick to the surface; small splash; even rhythm.

Back Crawl Sequence

50

Arm Action

a) Demonstration of the whole stroke with comments on the arm action.

b) Attempt the whole action.

c) Push off from the pool-side kicking strongly, with or without sculling, to obtain a correct body position, then introduce a windmill type action of the arms.

d) Having established a correct body position and a good leg kick, use a single arm action, for a short distance, with the other arm held alongside the body or extended beyond the head.

e) As in d) changing arms at appropriate intervals.

When the swimmer is performing the bent arm action, the teacher should encourage a positive rolling action. This permits the muscles around the shoulder to work at a favourable angle when the hand is at its highest point at the beginning of the push phase. It also lifts the opposite shoulder and arm clear of the water during recovery.

It should be noted that practices using arms only are not suitable for beginners and they are not recommended for general use.

If a rail is available, one foot may be hooked under with the other foot placed flat against the wall below, and the arm movements practised.

If there are great difficulties in attaining the correct entry position, some manual guidance may be given.

If there is great difficulty with the arm action the pupil may stand in water at chest level, to perform the pull-push. The head should turn to allow the pathway of the movement to be observed throughout.

Points to emphasize are: maintenance of propulsion through the push phase; straight and relaxed arm through recovery to entry; entry with little finger first.

Co-ordination

Demonstration of the whole stroke with appropriate comments which will be repeated during practices across the width of the pool.

Points to emphasize are: continuous action with one arm directly opposite the other throughout: regular timing with three leg beats to each arm: avoidance of pauses: encourage the feeling for a smooth rhythm.

Faults	Causes	Corrections
1) Hips too low	a) Head too high. b) Body position misunderstood.	a) Back of head and ears in water – look upwards. b) Lift tummy to surface – feet flat.
2) Legs too low	a) Head too high. b) Weak leg kick.	a) As 1a) above. b) Legs only practices – full swing from the hips – avoid bending knees.
3) Lower legs coming out of water	a) Trying to swim faster by kicking too strongly with insufficient control. b) Hips too high.	a) Kick with straight legs. Glance downwards to observe toes dimpling water surface. b) Adjust the head position. Kick with straight legs and observe. c) Practise leg action holding a float over the knees.
4) Cycling	a) Lack of appreciation of correct action.	a) Kick with straight legs and observe. b) Practise leg action holding a float over the knees.
5) Flutter kick	a) Lack of appreciation of correct action.	a) Slower and deeper kick with stress on action from the hips.
6) Kicking with feet dorsi-flexed	a) Lack of appreciation of foot position. b) Lack of mobility in ankle joint.	a) Kick with toes pointed; press upward with instep. b) Emphasize arm action, using legs mainly for balance. c) Ankle loosening exercises.
7) Hands entering too wide	a) Lack of appreciation of entry position. b) Lack of shoulder mobility.	a) Use exaggerated entry position i.e. on or over the centre line of progression. b) Swing the arm over the shoulder. c) Shoulder mobilising exercises
8) Hands stopping at thighs	a) Failure to appreciate the windmill action.	a) Stress the alternating action rather than one arm following the other. b) Stress continuity of movement without pauses.
9) Back of hand entering water first	a) Lack of appreciation of hand position. b) Lack of mobility.	a) Land and water exercises attempting rotation of the arm to obtain little finger entry. b) Shoulder mobilising exercises
10) Bobbing	a) Too deep an armpull.	a) Practices with emphasis on shallower pull.

Reader's notes

Chapter 8

Front Crawl

The Front Crawl is the most mechanically efficient of all strokes because the body is in a position in which force can be directed mainly backwards, powerfully and continuously with the minimum of retardation. This results from an alternating arm action accompanied by a leg action which helps to balance and maintain the body in line. It is mechanically more efficient because it places the strong muscles of the chest and shoulders in the best position to exert a pull in the direction that will produce the most effective reaction.

The Front Crawl is usually the stroke used in Freestyle races, the terms being considered synonymous nowadays. In many places it is the stroke which is taught first although it can present difficulties to some beginners. To swim it correctly the face has to be in the water for most of the time so that breathing must fit into the stroke without upsetting the balance of the streamlined body position and the rhythm of the limb movements. However, if the confidence practices (outlined in Chapter 5) have been mastered, learning the Front Crawl should not be too difficult.

Following a demonstration by a competent swimmer, initial attempts at the whole stroke should be made, with the face in the water, head held steady, and with the eyes open and looking forward-downward. The distances attempted at this stage should be short. Development of the stroke should be in the order previously suggested (Chapter 4) body position, leg action, arm action, breathing and timing. Each stage should be as efficient as the capability of the performer, at the time, will allow.

Body Position
The body lies almost horizontal, at the surface of the water with the head being neither raised nor lowered, but in line with the body, the eyes looking forward-downward. In this position, the water surface will be somewhere between the eyes and the hairline. The position of the head is important. If raised it will cause the hips and legs to drop, thereby increasing the resistance to forward motion. If the head is lowered into the water (eyes looking straight down) the hips will be raised and the leg kick could be less efficient.

The physical make up of individuals will affect the ideal position and with poor floaters the teacher needs to develop an efficient leg kick which will produce and maintain a stable body position. This in turn will allow necessary head movements to be made when breathing.

The most suitable head position having been found, its movement should be confined only to the action of inhalation which should be completed with the minimum, if any, interference with body balance.

The necessary and unavoidable rotation which takes place around the longitudinal axis of the body allows the strong muscles of the chest and shoulders to act in the most effective manner.

Leg Action
The leg action is basically an alternating up and down kick, suggesting movement in the vertical plane. This however is not strictly true.

As the body rotates the hips and legs will move similarly and kicking will take place first to one side (a) then to vertical (b) then to the other side (c) (fig. 8·1).

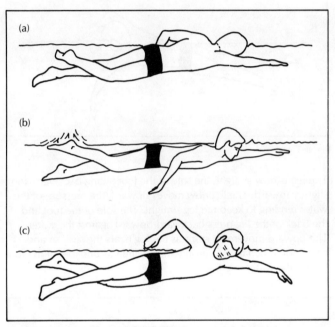

Fig. 8·1

This action is exaggerated in swimmers who roll excessively, by reason of immobile shoulders or difficulty with inhaling in the trough (fig. 8·2).

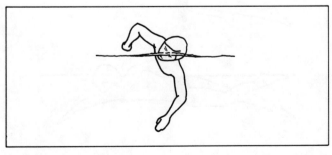

Fig. 8·2

The downward kick (fig. 8·3) starts in the hip, (a) using the strong muscles of the thigh, and travels through the knee, (b) which bends slightly from the pressure of the water. At this stage the thigh stops its downward movement (c) and the strong muscles in the front of the thigh contract and straighten the leg. The foot is extended to allow largest possible area of the instep and outer area of the foot to bear upon the water, thereby bringing about forward reaction from the backward-downward pressure.

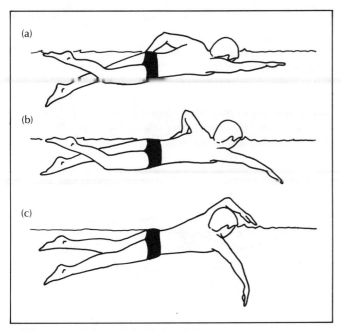

Fig. 8·3

The leg is now straight, the sole of the foot facing backward and slightly inward. The leg now moves upward, the pressure of the water tending to keep the leg straight. The sole of the foot and the back of the leg press backward-upward against the water. The upward movement stops as the leg nears the surface and care should be taken to ensure that as little as possible of the foot breaks the water (fig. 8·4).

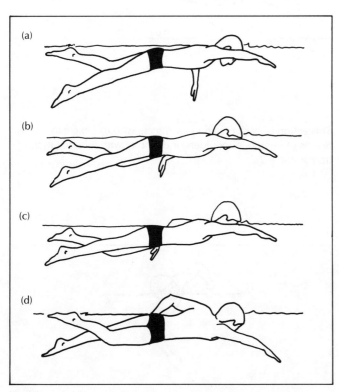

Fig. 8·4

The ankles remain flexible in preparation for a smooth transition to the next downward kick with an extended foot.

The legs should pass as close as possible to each other in a smooth continuous action. As one leg finishes the upward kick, the opposite leg is at its lowest point. The kick is usually contained within body depth, usually between 30cms and 45cms (12-18 ins). This helps to keep retardation to a minimum and to keep the thrust of the legs behind the body.

If the swimmer lacks flexibility in the ankles then the efficiency of leg kick will suffer, and may even cause retardation. Swimmers with large flexible feet, good mobility in the ankle joint, together with strong thighs, should develop a kick that will aid propulsion as well as maintaining a flat streamlined body position.

If ankles are stiff, the aim of the teacher should be to produce in the swimmer, a kick that has a balancing action which will maintain a reasonably good body position, and then to concentrate more on the arm action.

Arm Action

The arms provide the main propulsive force and the complete action is basically alternating and continuous.

Entry

The hand enters the water in advance of the head on its own side of the body centreline. Ideally, the entry position will be confined to a position between the centreline to a point in line with the shoulders. An entry outside the shoulder width or crossing to the opposite side of the centreline should be considered undesirable.

The arm is not fully extended but sufficiently flexed at the elbow to allow a downward slant from the elbow to the wrist. The hand can be in line with the forearm or slightly flexed. The fingertips enter the water first followed by the wrist and then the elbow. The hand continues to move forward and slightly downward feeling for the 'catch' position which occurs approximately

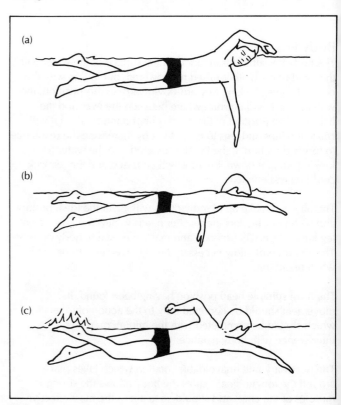

Fig. 8·5

15cms (6ins) below the surface (fig. 8·5(b)). This is the point where the shoulder will begin to roll toward the pulling arm to place the hand in the most mechanically advantageous position to start the pull.

Some swimmers will be seen to enter the hand with the thumb first, but teachers should encourage beginners to make the entry with fingertips first and with palms facing backward.

Propulsion
Pull Phase. The limb track is so directed to obtain a mainly backward force. Having gained a purchase on the water the hand exerts a downward-backward pressure at the start of the pull, which changes to a mainly backward direction, and with the wrist held firm, the hand leads the elbow (fig. 8·6).

At first the pathway tends to travel outwards, then inward towards the centre line, as it comes level with the shoulders. There is little variation in the depth of the hand which will be determined by the angle at which the elbow is bent and this can vary from a right angle to almost a straight line. Factors which can influence the degree of bend are strength, the amount of roll and/or personal preference. Swimmers should be encouraged to use a bent elbow which will provide a more effective leverage than a straight arm drive.

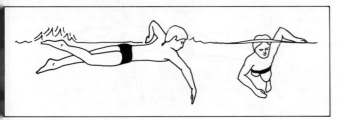

Fig. 8·6

Push Phase. This part of the propulsive phase starts when the hand and elbow are in line with the shoulders. The hand is near to the centre line, and the body roll at its maximum. The hand should continue to press backward toward the thigh, the wrist

Fig. 8·7

being adjusted to keep the hand facing backward. The shoulders start to return to the horizontal position and the hand continues to press backward whilst moving outward until it is alongside the thigh, with the arm being fully extended before the recovery starts (fig. 8·7).

The teacher should encourage a long push in the learning stages of the stroke and discourage the turning of the hand, to allow the little finger to lead during the final effort.

It is accepted that distance swimmers will normally use a longer push phase than the sprinters, who will tend to recover the arm earlier, before it is fully extended.

Recovery
The transition from propulsion to recovery should be smooth and continuous. The arm should be lifted from the water with the elbow leading. This movement is aided by the leaning over of the shoulders as the opposite arm moves into its pull phase. The elbow is kept high as the arm continues to move forward in a fairly straight line. The hand passes close to the head as it is taken forward toward the entry position. The whole action should be controlled with the minimum of tension (figs. 8·8, 8·9).

Since an outward, swinging, semi-circular action will upset the balance of the body, it should be avoided unless the physique of the swimmer prevents the use of a high elbow during recovery.

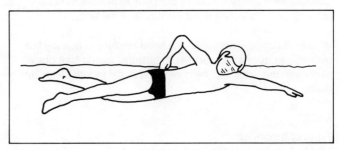

Fig. 8·8

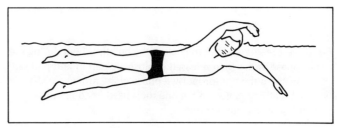

Fig. 8·9

Breathing
The act of breathing requires the head to be turned so that the mouth clears the water but, in so doing, it can upset the balance of the body from the normal streamlined position.

Therefore, any additional movement of the head should be avoided so that there is the least possible interference with the complete action of the stroke.

The head can be turned to either side to inhale. The preferred side may not be the best, and the teacher should encourage pupils to inhale on the side which maintains the best body position, and to practise breathing skills until they are able to breathe on either side, with equal ease.

The timing of the breathing is very important and it must be fitted into the stroke at the correct point.

Inhalation takes place as one arm is about to start the pull and the elbow of the arm on the breathing side is about to start the recovery (fig. 8·10).

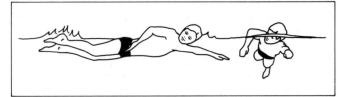

Fig. 8·10

There will be slight variations in the timing, depending upon personal preference, the most common of these being to breathe slightly later e.g. under the arm, but in any event the complete action should be performed as smoothly as possible.

The speed at which the swimmer is moving will determine the amount of head turning required to clear the water. When swimming quickly, the head will create a bow wave and the in-breath can be taken in the resulting trough, which will be slightly below the general surface of the water. If moving very slowly, little or no bow wave is created and the head needs to be turned further for inhalation to be possible. This can create undesirable re-actions, causing the body to twist or to bend sideways, thus affecting the streamlining of the body.

When inhalation is complete, the head is returned quickly but smoothly to its original position. Exhalation should take place partly into the water and be completed as the mouth clears the water.

Types of Breathing
Trickle Breathing. As the head is returned to its normal position after inhalation, the breath is slowly exhaled through the mouth and nose into the water. The exhalation is controlled to allow the inhalation to take place at the non-propulsive phase of the arm cycle i.e. during recovery.

Explosive Breathing. After inhalation the breath is held during the major phase and is then released explosively part in and part out of the water at the non-propulsive phase of the arm cycle. This type of breathing pattern is the one most used in competitive swimming, especially sprinting.

Breathing Patterns
Unilateral Breathing. Breath is taken, by any method on the same side throughout the swim.

Bilateral Breathing. Breathing takes place every one and a half stroke cycles thus breathing to alternate sides. This method adopts a pattern, for example, of taking a breath as the right arm is about to recover, the left arm pulls, followed by a right arm pull, with the next breath taken on the opposite side as the left arm completes the pull and is about to recover. The trickle or explosive method may be used with this pattern of breathing.

Breath Holding is the term used to describe a technique where the breath is held for several strokes. This method is used when teaching beginners the Front Crawl stroke, to allow them to concentrate on obtaining a good style. It is often used by the sprinter who will breathe only occasionally in the early stages of the race, later increasing the rate, perhaps to one breath per stroke cycle, and finally holding the breath for the last few metres toward the end of the race.

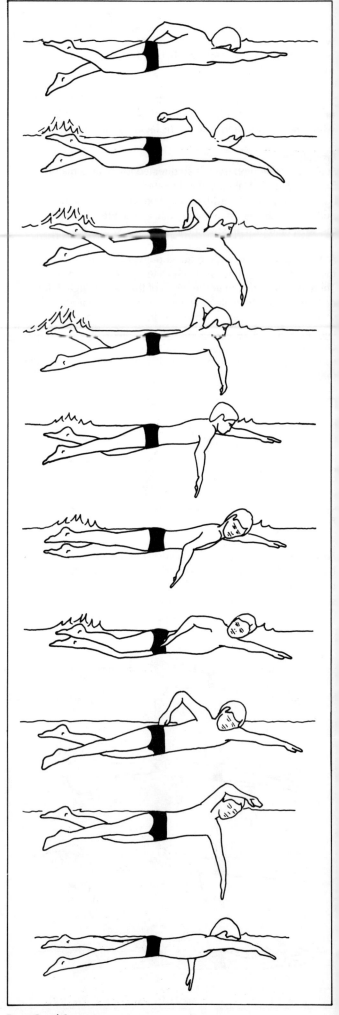

Front Crawl Sequence

Co-ordination

The co-ordination of leg and arm actions usually occurs quite naturally. Most commonly, six beats of the legs are made during one arm cycle, with the opposite foot kicking downward at the beginning of each pull. The six leg beats are not always of the same depth, producing perhaps two major kicks and one minor kick. Sometimes the minor kick may be so small as to produce a four beat action. In some instances the swimmer may adopt a two beat kick, the legs being used only for balance.

Variations

Physique, strength and flexibility, related to stroke mechanics, will produce variation of style. A good teacher will take note of such variations in individuals taking utmost advantage of the positive elements, then making any necessary adjustments.

Strong Arms/Shoulders. Swimmers with strong, flexible shoulder girdles reveal a more pronounced roll as they apply the most effective leverage on the water. This in turn will cause the hips to roll more than usual. The resulting re-action of the legs against the body swing may cause them to cross over. This kick can be equally as efficient as a kick in the vertical plane. Another variation with such swimmers is one in which faster stroking rate of the arms is used with the legs producing mainly a balancing effect.

Stiff Shoulders. Swimmers who lack mobility in the shoulder girdle may adopt one of the following variations to overcome this deficiency:

a) An arm recovery which is flat and wide, often resulting in an entry outside shoulder width and an early recovery.

b) An arm recovery, flat and wide, with a flinging action which will result in excessive lateral deviation of the body when trying to achieve an entry close to the centre line.

c) A deep arm pull or one which crosses the centreline. This is caused by attempting a high elbow recovery resulting in a body roll approaching 90°.

Weak Arms/Shoulder Girdle. The most common feature with this type of swimmer is the loss of purchase on the water, as a result of leading with the elbow, having a loose wrist and a wavy pathway.

Stiff Ankles. Kicking with stiff ankles will cause retardation with the wasting of valuable energy. If the stiffness is inherent a stroke will develop in which the propulsive power of the arms is emphasised, with the legs merely producing a balancing effect.

Teaching the Stroke

The same procedure is followed as in teaching other strokes. First of all there should be a good demonstration by a competent swimmer with brief comments on the salient points given by the teacher. Then the pupils should be allowed to attempt the whole stroke. Non-swimmers, using artificial aids may try likewise, although if they are able to regain standing position from a push and glide in the prone position, artificial aids may not be necessary, provided that the water is shallow. It must be stressed that attempts at the full stroke should not be hurried.

Part practices should now follow in the sequence of legs, arms and breathing, interspersed with full stroke practices emphasising good poise and continuity of movement.

The greatest difficulty in learning Front Crawl is the mastery of the breathing technique. For this reason it is strongly recommended that beginners should first concentrate on developing a good style over short distances, concentrating on the arm and leg actions whilst holding the breath. Although the following practices can be used in learning Front Crawl it should be pointed out, that the teacher need not use all of them because the needs of individuals or groups will vary. Some stages may not even be required in order to progress to the full stroke. Times spent on each practice may differ, one requiring more stress than another.

Teaching Practices and Teaching Points
Full Stroke Practice

Following a competent demonstration with comments the pupils enter the water and attempt the stroke, with the face in the water and holding the breath. This allows concentration on the leg and arm movements only. Careful observation by the teacher will decide what practices are required.

Teaching Points
Body position – flat, horizontal, streamlined; head in its natural position, face in the water.

Leg Practices

a) Recapitulation – push and glide with emphasis on poise (fig. 8·11).

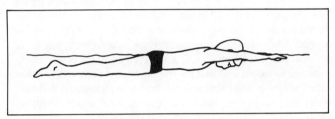

Fig. 8·11

b) Push and glide adding leg kick, gradually increasing distances (fig. 8·12).

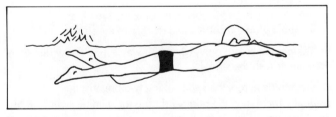

Fig. 8·12

c) Practise at side of pool holding the rail or trough. This enables the teacher to assess ability and advise where necessary.

d) Practise with a float held at arms' length. The less confident may require a float under each armpit but beware the poor body position which may be caused. Beginners need encouragement to make a small splash with the feet, to prevent the hips and legs from being too low.

Teaching Points
Swing from the hips; make long legs; legs straight and close together; loose ankles; toes pointed; small splash only; continuous movement.

Arm Practices

a) A reasonable degree of proficiency in the leg action having been achieved, and following a quick demonstration of the full stroke, with comment on the arm action, the whole stroke should be attempted.

b) Standing with one foot in advance of the other, leaning forward with shoulders in the water, pupils copy the teacher's demonstration with emphasis on entry, catch, pull, push and recovery.

c) Attempt the whole action with the face in the water.

d) Attempt the same action whilst walking.

e) Push and glide from the side of the pool, add leg kicks to establish a good body position then add the arm action for the remainder of the distance to be covered.

f) Repeat e) reducing the number of the preparatory leg kicks and increasing the distance using the arms.

Teaching Points
Hand entry between shoulder and centreline; fingers enter first, followed by wrist and forearm; 'catch' about 15cms (6ins) underwater; pull under the body with elbow flexed, push to the thigh, palm facing backward; recover the arm with a high elbow; maintain continuity of movement.

Care should be taken in the use of buoyancy aids which should be dispensed with as soon as possible.

The use of the 'arms-only' practices, using buoyancy aids for the legs, should be confined to the advanced training of skilful swimmers and it should be noted that unless an aid provides support similar to that given by the leg kick a different body position will result, which will affect the limb track of the arms. It should be noted also that the use of inflated rings will interfere with the arm action causing a pull and recovery which will be wider than necessary. Arm bands, especially if fully inflated, will cause difficulties in the pull and push phases of the stroke. An efficient leg kick will reduce the dependence on artificial aids, the use of which should be avoided if possible.

Breathing Practices
a) Short practices of full stroke, holding the breath and concentrating on the pattern and rhythm of the stroke.

b) Taking one breath only, when half way across the width, then continuing with the stroke.

c) Swimming across the width taking two breaths, then gradually increasing the number during succeeding swims, until one breath per cycle is achieved.

d) If difficulty is experienced, practices whilst standing in shallow water can be tried. The shoulders and face should be in the water. One arm should be held forward as if reaching for the 'catch' position with the arm on the breathing side held close to the hip as if to start the recovery. The head is then turned as in the full stroke practice. Emphasis should be placed on turning the head to inhale so that only the mouth is clear of the water, and returning the head to its forward position with an unhurried action, to exhale into the water.

e) The same breathing action d) can be practised while holding the rail or trough and performing the leg action.

Teaching Points
Head turned and not lifted; breathe out partly into the water and partly as the mouth clears the water; breathe out forcibly; breathe in as the recovering arm leaves the water, the head turning to that side; return the head to its forward position as soon as possible; make the whole movement smooth and unhurried.

Co-ordination – Timing
As the pattern of the whole stroke is established, including the breathing, distances to be swum can be increased. Emphasis should be placed on good style, economy of effort and the establishment of a smooth rhythm.

At first swims should be short, with the teacher moving around observing and giving individual advice and encouragement. Individual part practices may be required to eradicate a fault or to remedy a weakness.

As style develops, not only can distances be gradually increased but other challenges can be added. In swimming lengths a swimmer can be asked to decrease the number of strokes required to cover the distance. By decreasing the rest interval between each swim stamina and endurance can be developed, until a set number of lengths can be achieved with ease.

Corrections
Before attempting to correct any fault it is essential that its cause should be found. This in turn requires that the teacher should be able to observe the movements taking place within the stroke and also be able to determine what has caused the fault and what corrective measures are required. Should there be more than one fault, the guiding principle should be to deal with the major fault first. For example, if a swimmer holds his head too high and his arm entry is incorrect (perhaps the entry is too wide) the aim should be to correct the head position (and thus the poise) before attempting to deal with the faulty arm action.

Sometimes the corrections need to be exaggerated. For example when the hands cross the centreline on entry, the teacher may encourage a deliberate placing of the hands wide of the shoulders. The swimmer, in attempting to follow this instruction will more often than not succeed in making an entry midway between the two positions, thus achieving a correct action. A more simple example might be to instruct a pupil not to splash, if the fault is such that he is bringing his feet out of the water.

Whatever the fault, the corrective practice chosen should always be related to the level of ability of the pupil. If, for example, a young swimmer has a weak kick at the early stages of learning he may need to be given two floats to hold, one under each arm, when attempting to correct his leg kick.

The maximum use should be made of good demonstrations to assist pupils to obtain a visual impression of the stroke. Only in rare cases should it be necessary to use manual correction.

Faults	Causes	Corrections
1) Head too high – resulting in an arched back and hips too low.	a) Fear of placing face in water; b) Mistaken idea of head position; c) Inability to master breathing technique. Incorrect breathing action.	a) Return to early confidence practices; b) Push and glide practices to establish correct head position; c) Full stroke practice for short distances without breathing.
2) Excessive turning of the head – upsetting body poise.	a) Turning the head from side to side out of water; b) Turning the head too high to breathe; c) Turning the head to look back when breathing.	a) Return to early practices; try bilateral breathing. Ensure that the head is turned to the side of the arm recovering; b) Full stroke with no breathing. Introduce breathing emphasising turning head just sufficiently for the mouth to clear the water; c) Use practices whilst holding rail or trough.
3) Feet or lower legs coming out of the water resulting in a weak leg action.	a) Head too low; b) Excessive bending of the knees; c) Poor ankle mobility.	a) Kicking practices with and without a float; b) Full stroke concentrating on legs and adjusting the head position to keep hips below the surface. Exaggerate by looking along the water surface; c) Kicking at rail or trough emphasise swing from the hip and extension of knee and ankle; d) Use exercises to mobilise the joint; e) Consider the need for greater stress on arm action with legs used mainly as balancers.
4) Shallow Kick (Flutter Kick) – resulting in a weak leg action.	Lack of feeling for the action required.	Kicking at rail or trough emphasize swing from hip and exaggerate the downward movement, Kick slowly and deeply.
5) Over-reaching at entry. Entry over the centre line causing lateral bend in the body.	Incorrect knowledge of the arm action.	a) Watch demonstration; b) Repeat earlier practices of arm action: (i) standing; (ii) walking; (iii) after introductory leg action; c) Exaggerated correction.
6) Flat/wide Arm Recovery affecting poise and hand entry leading to incorrect catch position and ineffective propulsion.	a) Incorrect understanding of Arm Action; b) Poor shoulder mobility.	a) Watch demonstration; b) Repeat earlier practices of arm action emphasising elbow lift, forearm below hand, reaching forward for entry with fingers first; c) Shoulder mobilizing exercises. If these are ineffective modify arm action to suit individual.
7) Lack of Propulsive power.	a) Incorrect pathway of the arms below the surface; b) Failure to 'pull' and 'push' strongly. Failure to apply the palm of the hand to the water or holding the fingers apart.	a) Watch demonstration, then copy demonstration standing in the water watching the path of the arm; b) Return to earlier practices: (i) standing; (ii) walking; stressing fingers together, palm pressing and pulling against the water.
8) Excessive Rolling.	a) Over-reaching at entry or pulling across the centreline; b) Arm recovery too high; c) Turning the head too far when breathing in; d) Poor balance due to ineffective drive; e) Pulling too deeply.	a) See 5) above; b) See 5) above; c) See 2) b) and c); d) See 4); e) See 7) a).

Reader's notes

Chapter 9

The Butterfly Stroke

Since it requires a high degree of strength, mobility and watermanship, beginners do not normally learn to swim Butterfly as early as other strokes. Indeed it is usually taught only to those who are already competent in the other strokes. Some teachers, needlessly, show some reluctance to teach the stroke, whilst others use it, in simplified forms, as a recreative activity in the early swimming lessons with a class or an individual.

Buoyancy is very important because the arms are recovered over the water and the head is raised to breathe. Good floaters will achieve this action with far less effort than poor floaters. Lack of mobility in the shoulder girdle may often contribute to a slow recovery of the arms and subsequent loss of swimming position. This, coupled with arms not properly clearing the water surface will create a resistance which grows progressively until swimming becomes impossible.

Therefore, it is true that bodily endowment will ensure success for some more than others. Nevertheless, all children should have the opportunity of attempting the Butterfly Stroke for, even if all do not achieve its mastery, the progressive practices can provide worthwhile experience in water.

Body Position
The body should be maintained as near to horizontal as possible with the head in its natural position, and the water level cutting its crown. The use of intermittent or alternate breathing assists greatly in maintaining this desirable swimming position. Undulation is unavoidable due to the reaction of the movements of the arms and legs. In a skilled swimmer the degree of undulation is controlled and minimal but in a learner it may be uncontrolled and excessive (fig. 9·1).

Swimming laws require that the body shall be kept on the breast with the shoulders horizontal when swimming the stroke in competition.

Fig. 9·1

Leg Action
Both legs move simultaneously, upward and downward, balancing the movements of the arms and the upper body. This gives rise to the forementioned undulating movement characteristic of the stroke (fig. 9·2).

At the end of the downward movement (fig. 9·3) the legs are straight with ankles extended and toes pointed, at a depth of about 50-60 cms (20-24 ins). The upkick starts with the powerful use of the hip extensor muscles and the legs move upward without bending in the knees. The soles of the feet press against the water, creating a force which is part vertical and part backward (fig. 9·4). The hips then start to drop, leading the upper

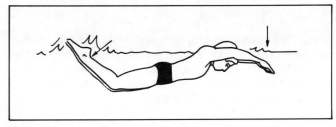

Fig. 9·2

Fig. 9·3

Fig. 9·4

leg in a downward movement with the knees bending, while the lower legs and feet continue to rise. This action continues until the knees are bent to approximately 90°. At this point some swimmers have part of the feet out of the water, but in all cases the ankles are fully extended (fig. 9·4). The lower legs then begin the propulsive thrust downward, a movement initiated by the powerful hip flexor muscles. As the legs thrust deeper, the hips rise until the movement is completed with the legs and feet fully extended and ready to begin another cycle.

Arm Action

The arm action is the main propulsive factor and, to be effective, strength and mobility of the shoulders are required. The arm movements are simultaneous and are continuous.

Entry: The entry is made with the hands in line with or just wide of the shoulders, the exact position varying with the degree of shoulder mobility (fig. 9·5).

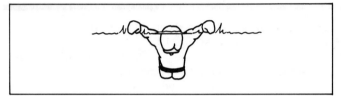

Fig. 9·5

The arms are almost fully extended, with the elbows raised and palms facing downwards. Often the hands are pitched at an angle which allows the thumb to enter first, with palms facing downward-outwards.

Catch: The catch is made as early as possible after entry, just below the surface of the water. It is made with the palms facing mainly backwards but, initially, there is a downward component which helps to raise the upper body and head. The elbows must be higher than the hands (fig. 9·6).

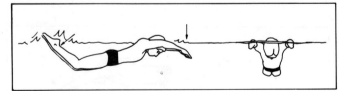

Fig. 9·6

At the start of the catch, inexperienced and weak swimmers may pause and glide while the legs continue to kick. As efficiency is gained, this undesirable pause shortens and should disappear.

Pull-Push: The pull and the following push phases provide the main propulsive force.

After the catch, the hands pull downwards, sideways and backwards until they reach a position about 30-45 cms (12-18 ins) deep (fig. 9·7). At this point the upper arms are in line with the shoulders. It is most important that the elbows are above the hands, which have now caught up with the elbows and are about to lead them as the push phase begins. In this high elbow position, the hands point downwards.

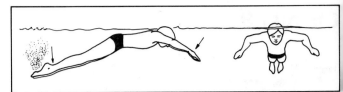

Fig. 9·7

The movement continues without pause into the push phase. The elbows bend so that the lower arms and hands move inwards toward each other while still pressing backwards towards the feet. At all times the hands lead the elbows. From the point where the hands are closest together, the elbows are straightened in a powerful and accelerating movement, with the positions of the wrists changing as the hands are pitched for the most effective propulsion (fig. 9·8).

Fig. 9·8

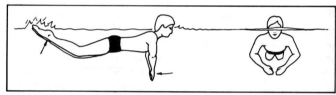

Fig. 9·9

At the end of this push phase the arms are fully extended as they sweep outwards to clear the hips for the transition into recovery (fig. 9·9).

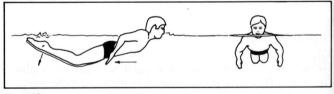

Fig. 9·10

The shape of the pull-push action is shown below:

Swimmers who lack flexibility in the shoulder girdle will use a V-pull. This has a wide entry and the first part of the pull is outside the shoulder line following a V-pathway, see below:

Recovery: As the hands and arms leave the water with palms facing upwards, they are carried sideways and forwards. Sometimes there is a bending of the elbow to aid the release of the arms from the water. The recovery movement is a smooth relaxed flinging action over the water. As the arms sweep past the shoulders, some swimmers have the palms turned down ready for a finger-tip entry, while others retain the thumb down position for the pitched entry already described.

Fig. 9·11

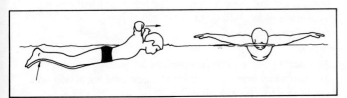

Fig. 9·12

Breathing

In Butterfly Stroke the explosive type of breathing is most frequently used. This involves a rapid exhalation followed immediately by inhalation. It is a technique requiring powerful use of the respiratory muscles.

As the arms are in the push-phase of their action, the head and shoulders begin to rise and some exhalation takes place underwater (fig. 9·10). However, the main exhalation occurs as the head and shoulders rise, until the mouth is clear of the water, with the chin pushed forward to lead the body. Forceful inhalation follows immediately and the breath is held as the head is lowered, to resume the streamlined swimming position, as quickly as possible, with the arms completing recovery.

The positions for breathing can be seen in fig. 9·10 9·11

Co-ordination

Butterfly is normally swum with two kicks to one cycle of the arms as illustrated sequentially in (fig. 9·13).

The first kick downward occurs as the hands and arms enter the water. During recovery, the arms having been in the air will have caused the hips to sink. The subsequent kick is required to be strong to balance the greater displacement.

The second kick occurs during the powerful and accelerating push phase of the arms. During this movement, the feet react towards the hands. This reaction will be proportionate to the strength and duration of the push and swimmers with a weak push phase will have a weak reaction.

The first strong kick and the second weaker kick are known as "major-minor". Should the second kick be a strong one, of equal force to the first they are called 'equal beat'. Both these actions have the common features that the first kick occurs when the arms are forward and the second kick when the arms are well back (fig. 9·10).

The distance forward or backward will depend on the personal factors of buoyancy, strength, mobility and skill.

Teaching the Stroke

In common with teaching all of the strokes the "whole-part-whole" method is considered best for teaching Butterfly (see Chapter 3).

Because the Butterfly Stroke is usually the last to be taught the following pre-requisites should have already been achieved.

1) Confidence, on the part of the pupil and the teacher.

2) Watermanship, such as the ability to keep the eyes open under water, to hold the breath comfortably, and to swim in a straight line, both under and along the surface.

3) The ability to move the arms simultaneously, and to move the legs simultaneously. This point is made because observation shows that some people are naturally symmetrical in their movements, adapting to Breast Stroke and Butterfly easily, while others tend to be naturally asymmetrical in their movements, and prefer strokes with alternating actions.

4) The ability to control breathing action as the face alternately leaves and enters the water. This is one of the reasons why many teachers say that sound Front Crawl needs to be established before attempting Butterfly. A swimmer lacking flexibility, particularly in the shoulder girdle, will almost certainly need to have much practice in Front Crawl breathing before concentrating on Butterfly.

Early Practices

1) Swimming Breast Stroke arm action with dolphin leg kick. Introduce this by asking pupils to imagine that their ankles are tied together.

Fig. 9·13 Butterfly Stroke Sequence

2) Bobbing up and down, submerging the face and the head and breathing when the mouth is clear of the water surface.

3) Swimming on the back with the arms sculling and moving the legs as though they are tied together.

4) Standing in shallow water and performing a standing dive over the surface to glide to the pool bottom, gathering the feet under the body, and springing into a second dive. Breathe as the face clears the water. Develop into a continuous series.

5) Standing in shallow water with arms extended forward at shoulder level and shoulder width, with palms down. Bobbing up and down and as the body rises from the water, pulling and throwing the arms strongly in a Butterfly action. Part of the pull will be through the water followed by a recovery through the air, thus giving a feeling for the movement ultimately required. This practice can be developed into a series of jumps in which the arms actually provide some propulsive force, with the pupil progressing across the pool.

6) Combining practices (4) and (5) by adding an arm action to each dive.

7) Swimming Butterfly with a Breast Stroke leg kick. Although this type of kick is not to be encouraged, it may be useful for the recreational swimmer who has very good Breast Stroke leg action to combine it with the Butterfly arm action. Normally, one arm action is co-ordinated with one leg action.

8) Practices may be performed on the back with or without sculling movements or with the arms performing an English Back Stroke action.

Leg Practices

1) Holding rail or scum trough, attempt 'Front Crawl' leg kick with knees and ankles together.

2) Repeat (1) emphasising knees and ankles together, feet extended. Kick by first bending the knees then whipping the lower legs downward with loose ankles. The feet should 'flick-flick' swiftly at the water. The hips should stay close to the surface.

3) Push and glide from the wall, on the front, on the back, or on the side. Extend the glide with a 'dolphin' kick. The arms may be extended forward or held at the sides. The hip movement should be emphatic.

4) With or without a float held out in front, push and glide from the wall and practise the leg action maintaining a streamlined position by keeping the face down and with minimal breathing.

5) Repeat (4) with the arms at the side.

6) Repeat and varying the depth of kicking with alternating shallow and deep kicks and continuous shallow kicks.

7) Without a float, with arms extended forward, push and glide into leg kicking. After a given number, a short Breast Stroke arm action should permit a breath to be taken and the kicking action to continue. There should be no interruption in the leg action.

Teaching points: Kick from the hips; drive down hard; maintain continuity of action.

Arm Practices

1) Standing with one foot forward, body bent forward, shoulders at water level, with arms extended comfortably in front of the shoulders. Practise the pull/push action and the over water recovery.

2) Repeat (1) with walking.

3) Standing about 2-3 metres from the wall with arms extended forward, with head down, pushing and gliding towards the wall and attempting an arm action.

4) Repeat (3) gradually increasing distance and the number of arm cycles.

5) Push and glide from the wall, adding arm actions.

During the above practices, the reaction to the arm action will bring about the same 'dolphin' type leg movement and an awareness of this will be of value when developing co-ordination.

Arm Action can also be practised as follows:–
1) Push away from the wall into a glide, add leg action and establish a two beat rhythm.

2) Push and glide-kick for four beats, include arm action with second two beats and finish with a short glide.

3) When practice (2) is established, increase the distance adding arm actions with each successive second two leg beats.

These practices are performed with breath holding.

Teaching points: Feel for the 'catch' and make the pull-push very powerful: ensure a relaxed arm fling in recovery: elbows higher than hands on entry: catch, pull and push; entry in line with shoulders: hands adjusted to maintain backward pressure during the pull-push: pathway of the arms close to the body requiring flexed elbows.

Breathing

1) As for arm practices (1) and (2) but incorporating breathing action as detailed in description of breathing.

2) Push off from wall and glide, keep the head down, establish leg action, add arm action with breathing as required.

3) Repeat full stroke increasing distance and breathing every second arm cycle.

4) Repeat, breathing every arm cycle.

Co-ordination

The Butterfly Stroke is very fatiguing for the beginner and a deterioration in performance will usually occur in the early stages of learning. It may be found helpful in the early practices to slow down the action by introducing a short glide after the re-entry of the arms following recovery.

1) Take a deep breath and with the arms extended in front of the head push off powerfully and glide, perform two leg kicks followed by one pull-push and recovery with the arms.

2) Repeat the push off and perform the complete cycle, two or more times, still with breath holding.

3) Repeat the push off, increase the number of cycles and introduce breathing during every second cycle.

4) Increase distance to a width, breathing in each cycle with emphasis on 'catch and kick, pull through and kick'.

Additional practices can include:

5) Push off and swim, using a fast continuous action without breathing.

6) Repeat, breathing at every 4-5 metres.

7) Repeat, breathing every second cycle.

8) Repeat, breathing every cycle

Teaching points: In the early stages, keeping the head down and breath holding will help achieve and maintain a flat body position: stress the first kick as the 'catch' is made: stress the second kick with the completion of the push phase of the arms and the start of recovery.

Faults	Causes	Corrections
Head high, hips low, legs low	i) Lack of awareness ii) Lifting head too high to breathe iii) Weak leg kick iv) Kicking from knees	Adjust head position. Push chin forward. Leg practices as needed. Revert to earlier practices which emphasise hip movement.
Excessive undulation	i) Dropping head and shoulders too low and too vigorously after breathing ii) Short or early entry of arms iii) Breathing too early	Using glide practices to flatten the body position. Revert to arm practices. Revert to earlier practices.
Head turning, shoulder dropping, twisting body	Faulty breathing action	Revert at once to earlier confidence practices. Arm practices incorporating breathing action.
Leg action Front Crawl or Breast Stroke type action in part or in total	i) Lack of confidence ii) Lack of skill	Revert to earlier practices.
Excessive knee bending	i) Lack of ankle flexibility ii) Holding the head up to keep the face clear of the water	i) Mobility exercises. Use another stroke to mobilise ankles. ii) Check that the eyes are open. Use rail and float practice to give feeling of hip movement. Start with upward kick with straight legs.
Small leg action or flutter kick	Inadequate movement of hip or knee bend	Emphasise depth of kick while using earlier leg practices.
No push phase	Recovering too early	Revert to arm practices stressing correct entry position & limb track.
Little push phase	i) Breathing too early ii) Lack of Strength	Emphasise breathing at the end of the push. Revert to arm practices stressing powerful pressure against the water from extended arm position.
Unequal push	Turning the head, or dropping a shoulder	Check the breathing action.
Arms hitting water in recovery	i) Lack of mobility ii) Low body position iii) Angled body position	Standing in shallow water, use a recovery emphasising elbows up and thumbs down. Check and correct the leg action. Check and correct head position and leg action.
Breathing too early, when arms are forward in the push phase	i) Lack of mobility ii) Using a gliding action iii) Weak push phase	Maintain continuity in the leg action – try to pull with the first beat. Use breath holding and check and correct push phase. Use breath holding while practising.

Reader's notes

Chapter 10

Starting to Dive

Diving is a natural development from activity in water. In order to swim, one has to get into the water and as confidence grows, enjoyment can be gained from different ways of entering, until progress is made to a head first entry. Diving may now be used either as a means of transfer from the pool-side to a swimming stroke or it may be developed as an activity for its own sake. Whichever way it goes, preliminary practices will be the same. In the early stages they will be concerned with the development of confidence and many of the practices will already have been used when learning to swim.

The practices given here are only a selection of many which could be used. Furthermore, it should not be assumed that all beginners will require the whole range. The more adventurous and able pupils will dive with very little guidance, whereas the timid child may take a long time to leave the pool-side. Practices should be selected in accordance with the needs of individuals and their previous experience. Whatever the situation, lessons should be enjoyable.

Early Practices in Water
Much of the introductory work in diving will be performed in the shallow end of the pool. It is important that the practices are not only leading to the performance of a head first entry from the pool-side; they should also relate to all aspects of diving activity, such as;

1) confidence under water, with eyes open,

2) the ability to regain feet and to surface,

3) breath control,

4) familiarity with rotation and the inverted position,

5) vertical thrust and extension of the body,

6) awareness of body shaping.

Submerging and Surfacing Practices
In all these activities, it is essential that the eyes remain open. Goggles should not be worn.

1) Wetting the face.

2) Blowing bubbles in the water.

3) Head bobbing under water, with the pupils holding the rail or standing freely in the pool. Pupils should be encouraged not to hold noses or, on re-surfacing, to wipe faces and eyes. A quick shake of the head is sufficient to remove water.

4) Mushroom float (See Chapter 12).

5) Swimming under floating objects placed on the surface, in a controlled area of the pool. Pupils are encouraged to move freely and to swim under any objects they meet.

6) Counting fingers. Working in pairs, the pupils submerge, to count the number of fingers shown by partners.

7) Picking up objects from the pool floor. Rubber bricks, coloured rings or any other clean objects may be used. Tin lids painted in different ways are useful for a variety of activities.

8) Touching the bottom of the pool with different parts of the body. The pupils should be encouraged to return to the surface by pushing from the bottom of the pool with both feet. This activity can be practised with a partner, either matching or making different body shapes. This encourages the eyes to be opened.

Stretching Practices
In all gliding activities pupils should be encouraged to push off evenly with both feet, aiming for the stretched body position to be used later for entries. It is essential for the head to be in line with the body, the upper arms to press against the ears and the hands to be held firmly together.

1) Pushing and gliding, on the front and on the back.

2) Pushing and gliding with roll over.

3) Revolving along the longitudinal axis of the body. This exercise can first be taught from a push and glide and then from a stationary floating position.

4) Pushing and gliding into forward or backward somersault.

5) Pushing and gliding to the bottom of the pool and re-surfacing by pushing away firmly with both feet.

6) Continuous surface dives, like a porpoise, around the pool. These can be practised alone or with a partner.

Springing and Rotating Practices
The main purpose of this group of activities is to encourage the pupils to use legs to gain maximum height and to experience being upside-down.

1) Springing high out of the water to show a fully stretched, streamlined position.

2) Springing high to make different shapes in the air.

3) Springing high, attempting to rotate around the longitudinal axis of the body, with the body remaining stretched.

4) Springing high and trying to get the shoulders to meet the water first on descent.

5) Springing high and trying to get the head to meet the water first.

6) Springing high and trying to get the hands to the place from which the feet started to push.

7) Springing into a handstand, with the head leading the body and aiming to get the hips over the shoulders. In the early stages, it is not important for the legs to be stretched. This will develop as skill increases.

8) Springing into a handstand, over a partner's arm held on the water surface. This may be attempted in forward, backward, or sideways directions.

9) Springing into the somersault from either a forward or a backward take-off.

10) Practising the plain header dive from a Y position stance in the water. In all these practices it is essential that the pupils should be made aware of the shaping of the body and the tension applied. This total body awareness is essential for progress to satisfactory diving.

Pool-side Activities

It must be stressed that diving is a deep water activity. Ideally, the water should be between 4m and 6m deep. For early practices a depth of 1½–2m is adequate according to the heights of pupils and the kind of activity to be practised. Before starting the pool-side activities, it is essential that pupils are confident to swim in the depth of water required. They may be quite confident in shallow water but apprehensive of working in deep water.

The following activities are suggested for progression to the Plain Header. Not all pupils will require every stage and the rate of progress will vary considerably with individuals. It is important that pupils are not hurried and they should be moved to the next stage, only when really confident.

Early Stages – from Pool-side into Water

It is important that pupils are quite competent in jumping from the pool-side before attempting to dive.

Feet First Entries

1) **Stepping** – to enter feet first, in tucked or stretched position.

2) **Jumping** – making different shapes in the air and entering the water with feet first and body stretched.

Tuck Roll

3) As in 2) varying the direction of flight.

4) Starting from a standing position on the pool-side with toes gripping the edge – springing high with body stretched and with arms upward on entry. Avoid leaning too far forward; looking down; pausing in take off. Ensure a powerful spring and a firm body on entry.

Head First Entries
The Tuck Roll
Crouch on the edge of the pool in a tight ball, with the body as compact as possible, head tucked in, hands holding the sides of the shins and, maintaining this position, roll into the water. Avoid lifting the head and losing the tuck. If difficulty is experienced, return to practices of rotation in shallow water.

The Crouch Roll
Crouch on the pool-side with the knees and feet together and the toes gripping the edge. The hips should be high. The arms should be pressed tightly to the ears and pointing down towards the water. The chin must be on the chest. Maintaining this position, roll forward and reach for the bottom of the pool. There is no push.

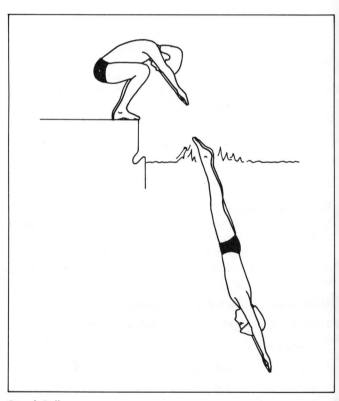

Crouch Roll

The Pike Fall
Stand on the pool-side with the feet together and the toes gripping the edge. The body is bent at the waist in a tight pike position. The arms are pressed close to the ears with the hands together. The head must be in line with the body, with the eyes looking for the point of entry. From this starting position, topple forward keeping the legs straight. Whilst dropping, the body is straightened for a streamlined entry. Avoid bending the knees and lifting the head.

The foregoing practices only require rotation by moving the centre of gravity beyond the line of the feet – NO push is required, and a head first entry is possible without concentration on the take off. It is important to maintain the starting position until the body begins to drop.

The following practices require co-ordination between a roll forward and a push from the pool-side.

The Crouch Dive
A similar starting position to that required for the Pike Fall is adopted. As the body begins to overbalance, a strong push is made from the feet up through the hips. A near vertical entry, about one metre from the side, should be encouraged. Avoid lifting the head and dropping too far before pushing. Reach for the bottom of the pool.

The High Crouch Dive
This is very similar to the previous practice but the stance is a little more upright. From this starting position, push vigorously through the hips, extend the legs and feet, and aim for a vertical entry.

The Spring Header
Once a good line through the air has been achieved this dive, which starts with a different arm position, can be attempted. Stand on the pool-side with the feet together, toes gripping the edge. A 'Y' position with the arms should be adopted. Care should be taken to ensure that the shoulders are in advance of the feet and the body held firm. From a slightly piked position, a vigorous drive is made through the feet, ankles, knees and hips. During the flight through the air, the arms and hands are brought together and the legs pressed into line with the body. Entry into the water should be with the body fully extended (see page 70).

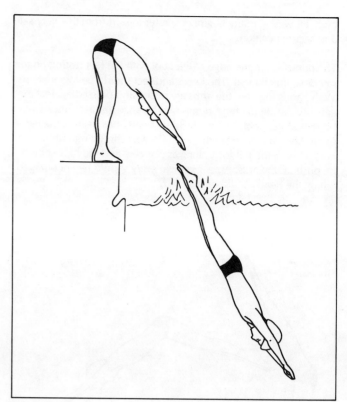

Pike Fall

Faults and Corrections
Faults for the foregoing dives will be obvious if the teacher is aware of basic principles and they can be corrected by appropriate comment or by returning to earlier practices if the faults persist.

In diving from the pool-side, lack of drive through the hips may be corrected by a pupil diving over a partner's arm held in front at knee height. As the push off is made, the arm is withdrawn. Care must be taken to ensure that the performer does not step back before take off, which can happen if the arm is held too high. Poles or other firm objects should not be used for this practice.

Additional Practices
Some pupils may experience difficulties in achieving a head first entry and the following practices may also be used. It may be necessary to include these with classes and larger groups, where the range of ability is wide and assessment of individual ability is made more difficult.

Sometimes, head first entries may only be achieved by using a one footed take off. For such practices, there is a tendency for a foot to slip and therefore, teachers should ensure that the pupils are gripping the edge of the pool firmly. These practices may also lead to pushing with one foot during subsequent practices. It is important, therefore, that a two footed take off should be adopted as soon as the pupil can make a head first entry.

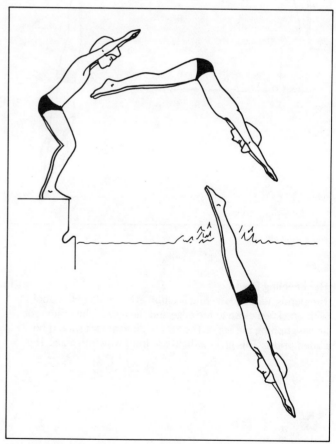

High Crouch Dive

The Sitting Dive
This is used by many teachers as the first progression with beginners but, with the increase in deck-level pools, it is becoming more difficult to perform. It also puts the pupil in a difficult starting position because the hips are low and the head

high. However, many beginners prefer to start from this very safe and secure position.

The pupils sit on the edge of the pool with the feet resting on the rail or scum channel. The knees and feet should be together. With hands together the arms are raised and pressed against the ears. By raising the hips, pupils overbalance and reach for the bottom of the pool. Once a head-first entry has been achieved, pupils should push from the side. The feet should remain in contact with the rail for as long as possible and the hips should be pushed upwards. A near vertical entry should be encouraged. Lifting the head should be avoided.

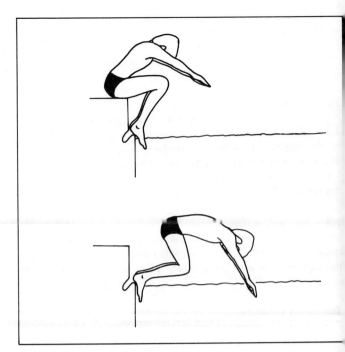

The Sitting Dive

The Spring Header

The Kneeling Dive

The Kneeling Dive
The pupils adopt a kneeling position at the edge of the pool, with one knee close to the edge and the toes of the other foot firmly gripping the edge. The toes of the rear foot should be curled under. This gives a firm base from which to push. The arms are stretched beyond the head and the body is bent forward until the shoulder touches the bent knee. The pupils now roll forward and ensuring that the head is kept well down, they reach with the arms for the bottom of the pool. As the body enters the water the legs should be stretched.

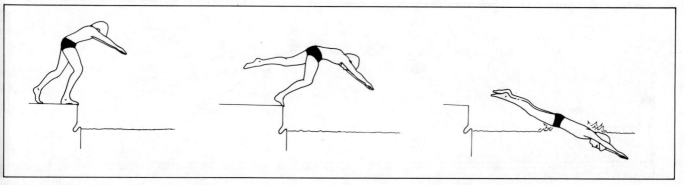

The Lunge Dive

The Lunge Dive

This is a progression from the kneeling dive. One foot is placed at the edge of the pool with toes gripping the edge. The other foot is placed about two feet behind. The body is bent forward with the arms and head in line with the body. The body now overbalances with the rear leg lifting. This leg acts as a counterweight and controls the rate of topple. As the hands reach the water, the front leg joins into line with the other leg. It is important to maintain the head position and avoid lifting the rear leg too vigorously.

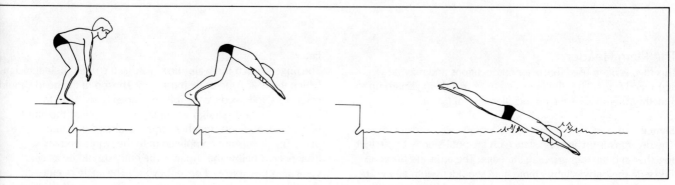

The Plunge Dive

The Plunge Dive

This dive can be readily adapted to suit the racing dive required for any prone stroke. It is often used as an intermediate dive between the Crouch Dive and the Plain Header, as a means of a head first entry in order to swim. The teacher has to decide whether to continue with practices having vertical entries, leading to formal diving or to introduce this dive which has a flat forward entry. In so doing, difficulties may arise when returning to vertical entries.

The dive begins from a crouched position on the side of the pool with the feet slightly apart and the toes gripping the edge. The knees are bent and the back rounded. The chin is lowered slightly to the chest, but the eyes look towards the point of entry. The arms hang loosely from the shoulders. The diver should feel balanced and relaxed. As the body overbalances and begins to fall towards the water, the arms are swung vigorously forwards in line with the body and at the same time there is a vigorous extension of the hips, knees and ankles. This extension should be taken right through to the toes. During flight the body should be streamlined. The entry should be at an angle of about 14° – 20° with the water. Fingers enter first with hands close together and palms down. The head should be between the arms and in line with the body for protection and to facilitate a clean entry. The streamlined stretched position should be held until the whole body is submerged then, by tilting the hands upward and lifting the head, the diver is enabled to return to the surface. It is important not to surface too quickly, for a sudden hollowing of the back can cause strain and form bad habits for the future. Full advantage should be taken of the glide to move smoothly into a swimming stroke.

Common Faults/Causes and their Corrections

Faults	Causes	Corrections
) An unbalanced starting position.	Standing on the toes – lack of firm contact with pool-side.	Check position of feet – slightly apart – toes over and gripping the edge of the pool.
) Falling too far before thrusting.	Misjudged timing. Hesitation in leaving pool-side.	Aim for a more distant entry. Thrust forward more suddenly – repeat until correct thrust is felt.
) Flat Entry.	Falling into the water; raising the head – both due to lack of confidence.	Return to earlier practices emphasising thrust, streamlining and reaching for the bottom of the pool.
) Hands apart on entry.	Lack of confidence in the extended position.	Return to earlier practices; exaggerated correction with hands together at take off.
) Slapping the hands on the water surface.	Thinking that this will prevent sinking.	Aiming at a particular entry point. Emphasise a firm streamlined body with head between the arms. Return to gliding practices.

71

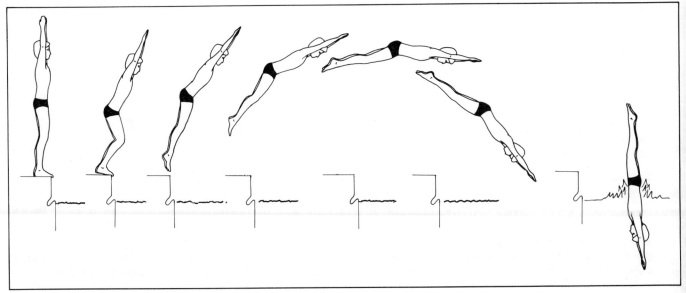

The Plain Header

The Plain Header

This dive is often used for minor competitions and may be performed from either the pool-side or from a diving board up to 3 metres. It embodies the correct elements of diving.

Stance

The diver takes up an erect stance on the pool-side with the feet together and the toes gripping the edge. The arms are raised in line with the body, slightly more than shoulder width apart. The palms should face forward with the thumb and fingers together. This is called the 'Y' position. The abdomen and buttocks should be pulled in and the chest lifted to give a firm, graceful position. There should be no undue tension in the body. The head should be in line with the body and the eyes looking forward. In profile, arms, shoulder, and trunk should be in the same upright plane as the legs.

Take-off

The take-off is probably the most important part of the dive, for this determines the line of flight.

From the take-off the diver must achieve height, distance and rotation. The rotation is achieved by driving up through the hips or moving the arms, head and shoulders down towards the water. At take-off, the knees bend and the shoulders move forward a little. Although the body is moving forward on to the balls of the feet, the hips must remain vertically over the toes. The knees straighten quickly and there is a vigorous extension of the feet.

The push must be directed upwards through the hips. Throughout the movement, it is important that the trunk remains firm with the arms in the 'Y' position. The arms should not be allowed to move forward and downward out of line with the trunk.

Flight

During the flight through the air, the body is bent slightly at the hips. The body follows a curved line of flight which is set on take-off. Apart from straightening for entry, there should be no other movements of the body during flight. The legs should be fully stretched with the toes pointed. Towards the end of the flight, the arms move together for the entry. It is important that the arms close against the ears. During the flight the eyes should be directed towards the point of entry.

Entry

The fingers touch the water first, making the initial hole through which the rest of the body must pass. The top of the head should enter next, followed by the fully extended body, with toes pointed. The body straightens out from its curve as the hands reach the water and stretches firmly towards the bottom of the pool. The dive is not completed until the whole body has disappeared below the surface. The entry should be as near vertical as possible and never beyond. The angle of entry can be altered by increasing or decreasing the degree of pike during the flight.

The Plain Header is only an introduction to diving and from here many pupils may wish to progress further. Most divers require a gradual build up of practices before attempting more formal and advanced dives. Progressive practices for these dives can be found in the book 'Diving Instruction.' Progressing from the Plain Header the following dives might be attempted.

Faults

Stance

Bad posture; head bent forward or strained backwards; back hollowed, knees bent; feet apart; arms out of line with the body; fingers apart; undue strain; complete lack of tension.

Take-off

1) Balancing on the toes and moving the body weight too far forward.
2) Excessive bending of the knees.
3) Moving too slowly.
4) Remaining too long with bent knees.
5) Lack of drive through the knees, ankles and toes.
6) Insufficient drive through the hips.
7) Leaning too far forward at take off.
8) Dropping the head & shoulders too quickly or too far behind.

Flight

1) Hollowing the back.
2) Excessive piking.
3) Lifting or dropping the head.
4) Arms out of line.
5) Opening the legs.
6) Bending the knees.
7) Lack of tension in the body.
8) Twisting the body.
9) Toes not pointed.
10) Hands not closing for entry.

Entry

1) Line of entry beyond the vertical.
2) Line of entry short of vertical.
3) Allowing the body to crumple on entry.
4) Hollowing the back and/or turning up the hands before the toes have submerged.
5) Arms parting from the pressure of the water.
6) Legs parting.
7) Entry with forehead and not the top of the head.
8) Arms moving together in front and not in line with the body.
9) Legs and toes not extended.
10) Body crumpling before it is fully submerged.

Corrections

These faults are caused by lack of awareness of the correct posture and may be corrected by good demonstration; verbal correction; practising the stance with the back against a wall; standing in front of a mirror.

These faults may be caused by lack of confidence or lack of understanding of the way in which the spring and the rotation are initiated.
Correct by a good demonstration; verbal correction, stressing, shoulders back, firm body and a vigorous push up through the hips; springing practices on the pool-side emphasising the drive through the knees and ankles; return to early practices in the water or from the pool-side.

Many of these faults are originated at take-off where the line of flight is set. Other faults may be caused by the diver's lack of body awareness. Corrections may be – a good demonstration; repetition of earlier practices with emphasis on pushing from two feet, driving through the hips and stretching the body; return to the Spring Header, ensuring good technique; verbal correction of individual points. In all corrections, concentrate on one point at a time.

The angle of entry is determined by the rotation imparted on take-off and the degree of pike during the flight. To correct these faults, it will be necessary to return to the High Crouch Dive or the Spring Header, with attention to the take off. Lack of body awareness will also be the cause of many of the faults and it will be necessary for the teacher to explain what is happening, dealing with one part at a time. Lack of confidence will require a return to earlier practices from the pool-side, aiming at reaching the bottom of the pool.

The Forward Dive with Tuck

The take-off for this dive is very similar to that used for the Plain Header. As the diver leaves the side, with the hips being driven strongly upwards, the diver tucks with the knees bent and the hands holding the shins. As the body descends, the body stretches for a vertical entry. Tuck jumps are useful practices for this dive.

The Forward Somersault with Tuck

The first practice for this dive is the Tuck Roll which was used to obtain a head first entry.

The diver can then attempt a somersault from a crouched position. The diver adopts a semi-crouched position with the arms bent and held behind the head. From this position, the diver drives strongly upwards through the hips and downwards with the arms.

During the flight, the body should be as compact as possible with the head tucked in and with the hands gripping the shins. Once the diver can achieve a feet first entry, progress to the complete dive can be made. The diver performs a similar movement to that used for the Crouch Dive, but starting from an upright stance. Initially, a rounded back may meet the water first, but gradually, with improvement a feet first entry will be achieved.

Reader's notes

Chapter 11

Starts and Turns

Although starting and turning are associated with competitive swimming, it is desirable nevertheless that these activities are included within any complete swimming programme.

The ability to perform efficient starts and turns will add to swimming skills and provide much satisfaction to those acquiring them.

Although some of the complete actions appear complicated, the component parts, in their simpler forms, can be used as contrasting activities during any lesson. The mastery of the basic skill of 'sink push and glide' on both the front and on the back is an important pre-requisite for learning turns. Front and back somersaults in the tucked and piked position will prepare swimmers for the practice of 'tumble' type turns, while sculling movements in a tucked position will help develop the necessary action required for a turning. Learning these activities will help to develop the required ability in body management combined with positional and directional awareness.

ASA Laws govern the manner in which strokes, starts, turns and finishes are performed. Teachers and pupils should be familiar with these laws which should be applied even in the teaching practices. To keep up to date with any changes, it is important that continual reference should be made to a current ASA Handbook.

Forward Starts

The Front Crawl, Breast Stroke and Butterfly races normally start with a dive from a starting block or the pool-side. Present ASA law states that the swimmer, on a signal, shall take up a position on the back of the block or stand a short pace back from the edge of the starting line. On the preparatory command 'Take Your Marks' the swimmer shall immediately take up a starting position on the front of the block or line and shall remain stationary until the starting signal is given. All these strokes have forward starts which are similar in application. There are several variations at advanced level, but the basic start described is the simplest to perform and it is usually taught first.

The Stance

In competition the stance is the position adopted by the swimmer after the command 'Take Your Marks' is given by the starter (fig. 11·1).

The toes should be curled over the front edge of the starting block or pool-side to obtain a good grip, thus avoiding the danger of slipping when the final thrust forward is made. The feet should be about hip width apart, to maintain good balance.

The trunk should be bent forward so that the shoulders are in front of the toes. The head position should follow the natural line

of the back and held comfortably with the eyes looking down. This position will vary according to personal preference or the physique of the swimmer. It is important that the body weight is finely balanced on the balls of the feet and indirectly this may affect the positioning of the arms. The position of the arms can range from slightly in front to a position behind the hips. The swimmer should now be preparing mentally for the need to react explosively to the starting signal.

Variations in the stance position which are commonly used are; 1) *the grab start* (fig. 11·2) which is often favoured by competitive swimmers and is easily identified by the manner in which the swimmer grips the front or sides of the starting block, with the hands.

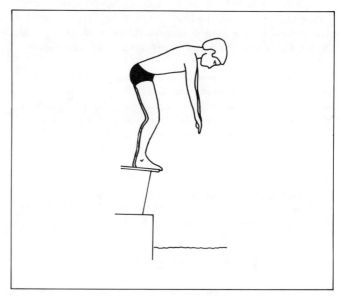

Fig. 11·1

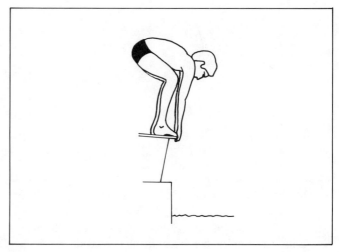

Fig. 11·2

2) *the track start* (fig. 11·3) which is used by some competitive swimmers has a stance similar to that used by sprint runners.

Fig. 11·3

Take Off

The angle of take off will affect the height of the flight and, consequently, the depth of entry. Variations are influenced by the stroke to be swum.

The flattest flight, shallowest entry and the shortest under water glide is that required for the Front Crawl stroke. When a longer glide is required, the angle of take off and the depth of entry are greater, thus allowing a longer under-water glide to take place.

The decision to take off is initiated by the starting signal, after which there is a movement of transition from the stance to a position which will allow a strong push away from the pool-side in the direction of the water. This movement is known as 'the drop', during which the arms perform a 'wind-up' movement by circling upward, backward and forward through 360°, in order to gain additional momentum from the swing.

At the signal, the knees bend and move forward causing the swimmer to overbalance. The arms begin to swing forward and upward and the head is lowered (fig. 11·4).

Fig. 11·4

When the arms reach the limit of the backward swing, the head is at its lowest point and the knees continue to bend with the heels raised (fig. 11·5).

Fig. 11·5

As the arms continue now to swing downward, the knees continue to bend to a right angle between the thighs and legs (fig. 11·6), the head starts to lift and the arms begin the swing forward with the body poised, ready to spring away (fig. 11·7).

Fig. 11·6

Fig. 11·7

The centre of gravity of the body is now well in front of the feet. Correct timing of the forward swing of the arms with the thrust of the legs is important to the mastery of the skill. The legs thrust

76

vigorously and the knees drive strongly to extend fully as the arms continue to reach forward. The head is lifted and the final thrust is made with the vigorous extension of the ankles. At this stage the swimmer takes a breath in readiness for the underwater phase of the start.

Flight
The body is now fully stretched as the feet leave the starting place (fig. 11·8). The head is then lowered causing a rotation of the body, the amount of which will affect the angle of entry (fig. 11·9).

Some skilled divers use what is called a 'pike entry', where the upper body is angled downwards for entry, while the legs are parallel to the surface of the water. As the upper body enters, the legs are raised to give a smooth entry.

Angle of entry is also affected by angle of take off.

Fig. 11·8

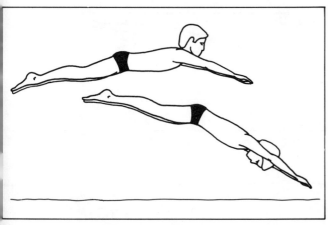

Fig. 11·9

Entry
The slight forward rotation of the body in flight allows the hands to lead the entry with the body maintained in a stretched position and as streamlined as possible (fig. 11·10).

The depth of entry is governed by the angle of take off and the control of the forward rotation of the body is caused by the lowering of the head. The angle of entry for Breast Stroke is deeper than that for the Front Crawl stroke in which the long underwater action is not so important. The Butterfly Stroke requires an angle of entry somewhere between the two.

Glide
The stroke to be swum determines the type of entry and the depth at which the glide should be held. A shallow entry and depth at which the glide should be held. A shallow entry and short glide are used for the faster strokes. After the body is fully submerged, the head should be lifted slightly and the hands pointed upwards to prevent the body from sinking too deeply.

The glide should be held while the body speed remains greater than that which can be derived from any propulsive movement of the limbs.

Fig. 11·10

Underwater Action

Front Crawl
As the momentum gained from the start is lost after the entry, and the glide slows down to swimming speed, the need to start swimming the full stroke will occur. The depth of the dive may be as little as 30 cms (12in) and as the speed diminishes the leg action begins, accompanied by one arm pulling, to assist the body to the surface where the full arm action can begin (fig. 11·11).

Fig. 11·11

The Breast Stroke
For this stroke the dive (fig. 11·12) is somewhat deeper than that for Front Crawl which will enable the swimmer to complete one powerful stroke with the arms following by a strong leg kick, while the body is wholly submerged. The timing of these actions is important since the law requires some part of the head to be above the surface before a second arm stroke begins.

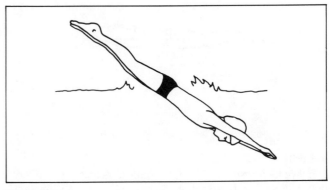

Fig. 11·12

As forward momentum from the glide decreases, the arms start the pull (fig. 11·13), in a flatter and wider pathway than normal, continuing with a backward push until they reach the thighs (fig. 11·14). This pull-push action is made as parallel as possible to the water surface, to avoid an undulating 'dolphin type' reaction from the legs, which could be mistaken for an illegal kick. The momentum from this powerful arm action will extend the glide phase, the body being held in the position shown. As the speed of the forward movement begins to decrease the arms are recovered, close to the body (fig. 11·15), and then pushed forward to an outstretched position (figs. 11·16, 11·17). At this stage the legs have recovered with the heels close to the seat to maintain an angle of approximately 120° between trunk and thighs, thus minimising retardation (fig. 11·17).

The swimmer then kicks and with a fine adjustment of the position of the head and hands the body drives strongly to the surface (fig. 11·18). The head breaks the surface and only then is the second arm pull started.

Note the following three important points in the underwater pull and kick.

1) The momentum gained from the dive, before starting to pull, should be fully exploited.

2) Full use of the momentum gained from the powerful arm stroke should be made before kicking.

3) The kick and the adjustment of head and hand positions should be timed so that the body drives powerfully to arrive at the surface to begin the first arm pull as the glide slows down to swimming speed.

These points will require emphasis during practice, in order to attain the maximum benefit from the underwater phase following the dive.

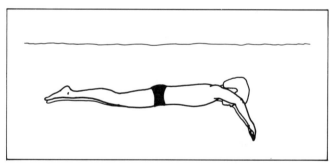

Fig. 11·13

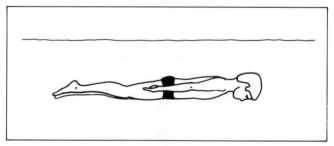

Fig. 11·14

Butterfly
The dive for this stroke is not quite so deep as that required for Breast Stroke but, nevertheless, the same principle of taking full

advantage of the thrust momentum should apply. It is important to note that for this stroke, swimming law requires that all movements of the feet shall be made in a simultaneous manner and although at the start and at the turn one or more kicks are allowed under water, only one pull-push of the arm action is permitted before surfacing.

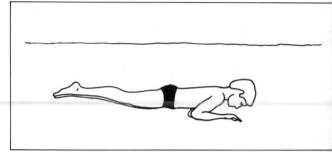

Fig. 11·15

Fig. 11·16

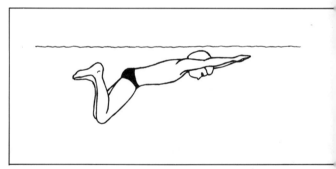

Fig. 11·17

Fig. 11·18

The underwater action comprises any number of simultaneous leg kicks together with one arm pull, similar to that in Breast Stroke, although the arms could pull deeper.

The 'dolphin' leg kick is a continuous movement which begins as soon as the momentum from the powerful arm action begins to decrease. It is used to continue the underwater phase and to help drive the body to the surface, for the arms to recover and the full stroke cycle to start.

Teaching the Forward Start

A well performed plunge dive (page 71) has almost all the action skill required for the forward start and is therefore, an essential pre-requisite. Two important aspects are the timing of the underwater transition from glide to first pull or kick and the transition from underwater to surface swimming.

The Plunge dive should be practised in order to achieve the maximum thrust from the pool-side, and an effective flight leading to a streamlined shallow entry. Proficiency is derived from practice, enabling the swimmer to produce a prolonged glide.

The transition to swimming should also be practised so that the swimmer may learn to assess underwater speed, to judge body position in relation to the water surface and the degree of adjustment required to effect a smooth transfer into the stroke.

Practices of sinking, pushing and gliding from the wall, then adding arm and leg actions, will allow these transition skills to be developed and mastered.

Having first attempted the whole skill, practices may now be introduced with an emphasis on good timing rather than on speed. By using the width of the pool more opportunity will be provided for practice, during which the pupils can make personal adjustments in the techniques being learned. Where use is made of demonstrations, it is important to direct attention to the underwater actions as well as those which are more obvious near the surface.

Once proficiency in the forward start is achieved, with modifications to suit the recognised strokes, competitive practice is a good way in which to stimulate and evaluate performance. Short races, which include the start sequences and a few strokes, will also be beneficial in acquiring the discipline of the starting procedures.

The Back Stroke Start

Present ASA Law governing a Back Stroke start states that; 1) Swimmers shall line up in the water facing the starting end with hands on the end, rail or starting grips. The feet, including the toes, shall be under the surface of the water. Standing in or on the gutter, or bending the toes over the lip of the gutter is prohibited. On the preparatory command 'Take your marks' the swimmer shall immediately take up a starting position, after which he shall not make any movement with any part of his body until the starting signal is given. 2) At the signal for starting and after the turn they shall push off and swim on their backs throughout the race. The hands shall not be released before the starting signal has been given.

Preparation

The swimmer, already in the water, faces the starting end of the pool, grasping the grips of a starting block, the rail or the pool-side. The arms should be in a comfortable position approximately shoulder width apart. The feet should be placed on the wall below the water surface. Some swimmers may find it more comfortable to place one foot lower than the other and experiments should be made to find which position is best suited to their needs. The body is held in this position without strain and the swimmer prepares mentally for the start of the race (fig. 11·19).

On the command 'Take Your Marks' the arms pull the body forward and upward towards the wall and the head moves nearer to the hands. At this point the legs are almost fully bent (fig. 11·20). The position adopted by the swimmers will vary considerably due to variations in their physiques and the positions and heights of grips above water level.

Take Off

On the starting signal the swimmer pulls on the hand grips and thrusts with the legs thus raising the body (fig. 11·21). The hands release their grip, the head is thrown back, and the arms begin to swing upward and backward. The legs are extended vigorously pushing the body into a shallow backward dive over the surface of the water (fig. 11·22).

Flight

As the legs are fully extended the arms are extended beyond the head and the body is stretched into a position as streamlined as possible (fig. 11·23).

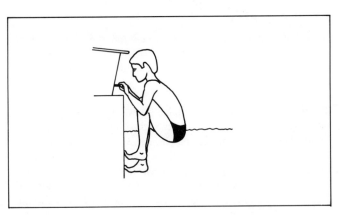

Fig. 11·20

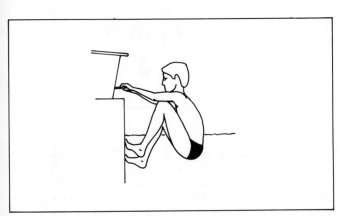

Fig. 11·19

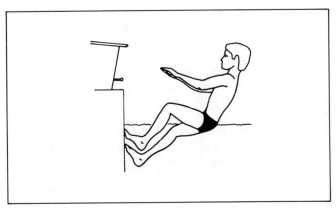

Fig. 11·21

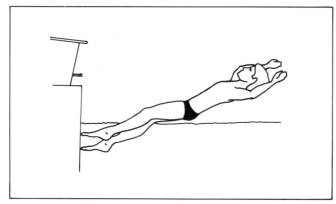

Fig. 11·22

Fig. 11·23

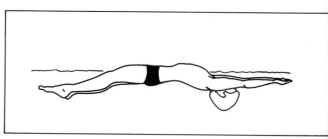

Fig. 11·24

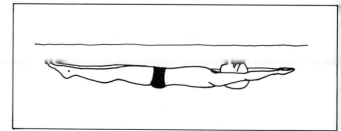

Fig. 11·25

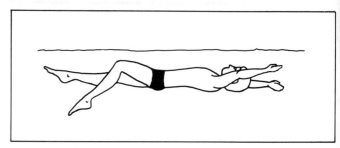

Fig. 11·26

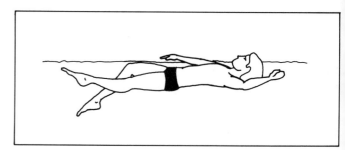

Fig. 11·27

Entry

The fingers lead the arms into a streamlined entry, the legs and feet remaining fully extended. The entry should be shallow and care should be taken not to sink too deeply under the water surface (fig. 11·24).

Glide

As with the front start the speed derived from the momentum of the take-off may be greater than the swimming speed. Full advantage should be taken of this, by holding the stretched body position (fig. 11·25).

The depth of the glide is controlled by raising or lowering the head. The leg kick begins as soon as the speed of the glide diminishes to swimming speed (fig. 11·26). By this time the swimmer is just ready to break the water surface. One arm pulls through to the side, with the other arm remaining close to the head in an extended position. The face is now above water and the normal stroke cycle begins with the recovery of this arm and the first pull of other (fig. 11·27).

Teaching the Back Stroke Start

The underwater phase may be more difficult to teach than that of the front start because the swimmer is less well orientated on his back. The practice of 'sink, push and glide' should be performed with the arms extended and held beyond the head in a stretched, streamlined position which is essential for the development of the whole skill. The practice should continue until the swimmer can control the speed and depth of the glide, judge his position in relation to the water surface and assess the degree of body adjustment required to effect a smooth transfer into the stroke. During the glide a slow exhalation through the nose will prevent water entering, thus avoiding discomfort.

The initial practices for the start also apply to the turn and if the following skills are mastered at this stage the task of teaching the turns will be much easier.

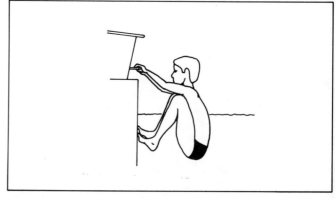

Fig. 11·28

1) In the water, holding the rail, scum trough or wall, adopt the position show in sketch (fig. 11·28).
2) Repeat 1 and leaving the feet in contact with the wall, roll backward (fig. 11·29) until the body is completely submerged, breathing out slowly through the nose to eliminate possible causes of discomfort (fig. 11·30).

3) When the 'back roll' can be performed easily and comfortably a push-and-glide is added. This practice is continued until an assessment can be made of the time to thrust with the legs.

4) Repeat 3 and adopt an extended streamlined body position resulting in a long glide at the correct depth.

5) Repeat 4 stressing the 'stretch and glide' to the surface (fig. 11·31). A competitive element may be introduced to see who can glide the furthest.

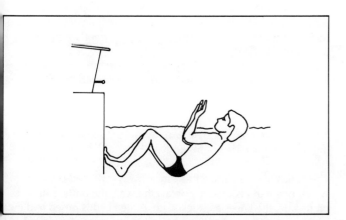

Fig. 11·29

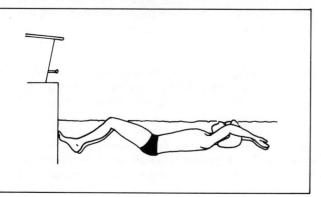

Fig. 11·30

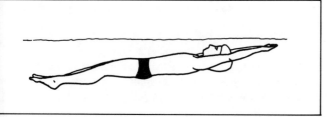

Fig. 11·31

When the underwater glide has been mastered the whole phase can be extended by adding the leg kick while the body is submerged, thus maintaining speed until the water surface is reached.

Control of direction might be difficult during the first few attempts and consideration must be given to class organisation when teaching these skills. To minimise or avoid collisions a class might be arranged in groups, to be set off in waves. All number ones are started and when danger from collisions are no longer present, number twos follow and so on. This method will also allow the teacher to observe more effectively and to comment on a more individual basis.

When proficiency in this exercise has been achieved, the transition into the full stroke can be practised. The timing of the first arm pull is critical and continued practice may be required in order to achieve success. As one arm starts the first pull (fig. 11·32), the opposite arm is kept close to the head in an extended position and it is held there until the first arm begins to recover (fig. 11·33). This recovery is withheld until the face is clear of the water and the practice ends with both arms fully extended beyond the head.

The teaching should always be preceded by a good demonstration with a commentary on the salient points. When possible, demonstrations using starting blocks should be arranged and followed by practice.

Practices should include experiment in the positioning of the feet on the wall to allow for differences in physique or personal preference. Practices in 'waves' or 'cannon' form can be used across the width of the pool.

After the attempts at the whole skill the class can be grouped according to ability.

Initial practices should include the backward dive, entry and the glide. Using a vigorous extension of the legs the body is pushed upwards and backwards co-ordinating with the arm swing to lift the buttocks clear of the water. Emphasis should be placed on the control of the head, which is thrown backward as the hands lose their grip. The back is kept slightly arched as the legs complete their thrust and the arms are quickly extended overhead to a position in line with the body. This can be achieved by throwing the arms through a pathway directly

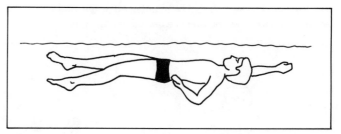

Fig. 11·32

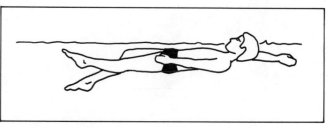

Fig. 11·33

Faults	Causes	Corrections
Pushing-off on the surface	Not rolling sufficiently under the surface due to lack of appreciation of the skill, or through discomfort caused from water entering the nose.	Return to rolling practices. Emphasise breathing out through the nose.
Push off too shallow	Lack of thrust resulting in failure to achieve the fully extended position with consequent lack of flight.	Push and glide practices with emphasis on thrust.
Push off too deeply	As for previous fault but with head too far back leading body into a deep dive.	As for pushing off too shallow.

upward–backward, or sideways–backward or a variation of these. Practice of this phase is essential until the entry is consistent and at the correct depth for the glide phase. When this is satisfactory the kick to the surface and the transition into the stroke can be added.

Faults	Causes	Corrections
Pushing through the water in a sitting position	Lack of confidence: and holding the head too far forward, chin on chest, and face out of water. Discomfort caused from water entering the nose.	Return to push-and-glide practices. Emphasise a backward head position. Use exaggerated correction – arch the back. Breathe out through the nose.
Entry too shallow	Push off-too flat. Feet too high on the wall. Not leading with the head.	Adjust position of feet. Stress the upward-backward arm pathway. Emphasise head back position.
Entry too deep	Over-extension of head position. Over-arching of the back. Exaggerated arm swing.	Control the backward throw of the head. Adopt the use of a wider, flatter arm action.
Feet slipping down the wall on take off	Feet too low on the wall. Trying the obtain height by pushing down.	Adjust position of feet to a position giving maximum purchase. Emphasise a strong backward thrust of the legs. Emphasise a head-back position.

Turns

In the initial stages accuracy rather than speed is more important. However, when turns have been learned, it is essential that they are practised in competition conditions which require performance at speed. As competence in any stroke develops the requirements of ASA law regarding the turn for that stroke should be emphasised. Part or even complete lessons might be devoted to turns. Using the width of a pool during a lesson will allow more practice to take place in a given time. The correct performance of turns should be encouraged from the earliest stages so that later, when distance swims are featured, the skill will be habitual.

There are basic factors which apply to all turns.
1)   Swimming speed should be maintained as the wall is approached to make the practice realistic.

2)   The turn itself should be as fast as possible.

3)   The feet should be approximately hip width apart on the wall to give a firm balanced base for the push-off.

4)   The body should never get so close to the wall that the knees have to be bent more than 20°, the optimum position for a powerful leg thrust.

5)   The underwater streamlined body position in the glide should be held firmly. The underwater swimming action and the transition into the full stroke should be performed as previously described for the start.

6)   The teacher and pupil should be familiar with the swimming laws applicable to the stroke and turn.

The Freestyle Turn
The Law governing freestyle turns allows the swimmer to touch the wall with any part of his body.

The easiest turn is named the 'throw-away' or 'head-up' turn in which one hand is used to contact the wall, the body is turned on its side, the knees are tucked up as the head is raised and the body swings in a vertical plane to allow the feet to be placed firmly on the wall. Simultaneously, the touching arm pushes the head and shoulders away thus assisting the rotation. The body sinks beneath the surface, both hands join together ready for the thrust of the legs and the ensuing streamlined extension of the body. This turn is sometimes called the 'grab' or 'pull up' turn.

The fastest and, consequently, the most often used turn in freestyle is the 'tumble' turn, which is not as difficult to perform as is generally thought. It is important for the teacher and the class to understand clearly what is involved before attempting it. The need to reverse direction whilst maintaining the maximum speed is important in competition. To achieve this, it must be remembered that the body's forward momentum has to be transferred to the opposite direction. Forward momentum is used to assist rotating movement and this is achieved by performing a forward somersault whilst holding the legs in a pike position for as long as possible, the head leading the trunk throughout. This movement should be almost complete before the feet are brought over the water and placed on the wall, ready for the push off.

The push off, glide and underwater action for this stroke has a shallower return to the surface than that in other strokes because the swimming speed is reached earlier in the glide . Therefore, to remain underwater for a longer period would be of no benefit.

Fig. 11·34

Teaching the Turns

Practices need to be adjusted to suit the space available and the size of the class. Ideally the pupils should be arranged to swim widths without obstruction. If space does not permit, initial practices may be carried out with the class divided into two lines, swimming from the middle of the pool towards the walls, to turn and return to the middle. Alternatively, the class may be arranged to swim in 'wave' formation, each wave starting when the first has completed two widths including one turn, or three widths including two turns.

The following early practices are useful.

1) Full stroke at speed, with a forward somersault once per width. This helps with orientation/awareness of body position in relation to the surface.
2) As (1), but add a second somersault with a swim in between.
3) As (1), including several somersaults – even two or three together.
4) As (2) with the second somersault performed close to wall to allow feet to be placed thereon.
An alternative to this could be pike jump towards the wall (fig. 11·34).

Practise at a distance from the wall performing a jump and a tuck.
Repeat close to the wall.

5) As (4) adding a push and glide from the wall on the back, and kicking to surface.

Teaching Points

Head leading – tight tuck, speed and momentum will aid rotation.
Keep tightly tucked.
Add a pike action on the approach to wall. Keep the head down.
Feet apart for a firm stance; hands brought close to the head; stretch into a streamlined body position.

When pupils are confident in these practices a 'half twist' can be introduced which will allow the swimmer to push into the glide in the prone position and therefore permit the transition into the full stroke to be performed smoothly.

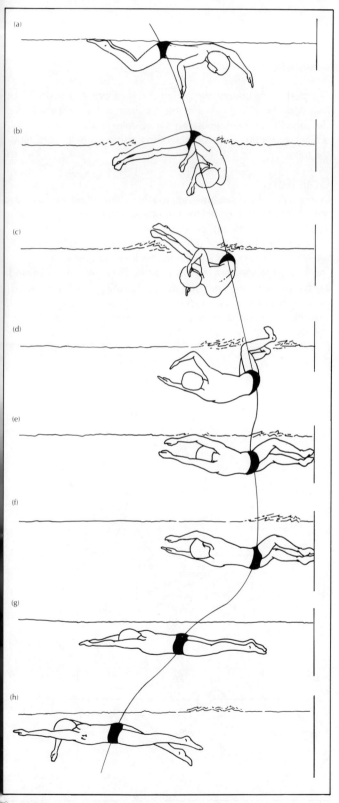

Fig. 11·35

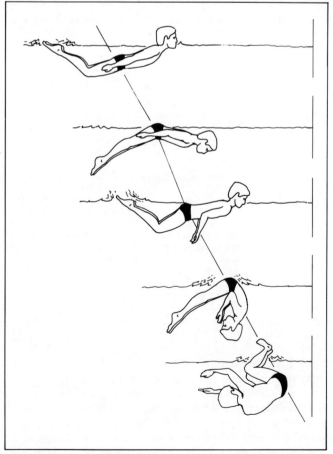

Fig. 11·36

The swimmer approaches the wall at speed (fig. 11·35(a)) and when about half a body length away the head leads the body into a piked position as one arm is about to enter the water in front of the head and the opposite arm stops at the beginning of the push phase. The head continues to lead the trunk whilst the forward arm is pulling to assist the roll, until it is in line with the other arm which has been bent while performing a sculling action to aid the rotation of the body (fig. 11·35(b)).

The legs are lifted and thrown over the water to the side of the forward arm (fig. 11·35(c)). At the same time, the shoulders are turned to place the body on its side, assisted by a sculling action of the hands (fig. 11·35(d)). The body continues to move forward during this rotation and ideally the feet will be placed on the wall about six inches apart with the knees bent to an angle of 20° (fig. 11·35(e)). As the feet are placed on the wall the arms will begin to extend (fig. 11·35(f)) and without pause a strong thrust of the legs will drive the body into a prone position during the glide (fig. 11·35(g)) and into the underwater sequence described in the section on Starts (fig. 11·35(h)).

In another commonly used turn, the swimmer will pull until both arms are in line with the body with hands at hip level. The leg action then changes to a 'dolphin' kick as the head leads the body into a piked position. The hands scoop forward-downward to assist rotation. The remaining sequence of movement follows the description of the 'tumble' turn previously described (fig. 11·36).

Faults / Causes / Corrections

Faults	Causes	Corrections
Inability to tumble smoothly and consistently	Inability to orientate the body in relation to forward direction, the water surface and the position of the wall.	i) Forward roll practices during swims. Pike jumps to somersault and place the feet on the wall. ii) Swim slowly into wall and somersault.
Push from the wall too deep; too shallow; to one side	i) As above, and beginning to turn too late and allowing the body to move too close to the wall.	Practise swimming into wall, at reduced speed, in order to turn. Increase speed gradually as skill improves.
Slow movement from the wall	i) Turning too early with the feet barely touching wall, resulting in a weak push off.	Practise for constant speed of approach. Use a marker on the pool bottom to judge distance.
	ii) Turning too close to the wall.	As previous practice with emphasis on re-adjustment of body position for push off.
	iii) Stopping the action too far away from the wall. iv) Loss of speed on approach to the wall due to raising the head.	Keep the head down and use bottom of pool to judge distances.

Back Stroke Turns

Performances of these turns may present difficulties, for swimmers cannot readily see where they are going. Present swimming law requires that the competitor must not allow the shoulders to roll more than 90° from the horizontal before touching the end of the course with head, shoulder, foremost hand or arm for the purpose of turning. Therefore, ability to judge distance becomes important in order to adjust the stroking

actions to position the body accurately for the touch on the wall. Both efficiency and legality depend on this judgement. Difficulties in judging distance can be overcome by having some kind of marker to assist in determining the relative body position. In competition conditions, this is achieved by having Back Stroke marker flags suspended above the pool and set at a distance from the turning ends. In the teaching situation such a provision may be difficult, so use should be made of other definitive points above the pool.

It is advantageous if swimmers can turn on either hand, although most tend to turn on a preferred side and will adjust the approach to enable them to do so.

The approach to the wall is the same for all turns and the faster it is, the faster will be the complete action when properly executed. A constant swimming speed is important in judging distance from the wall.

The push-glide underwater action and transition to full stroke following the actual turn and the transition to the full stroke is described in the section on the Back Stroke Start. It is an advantage if pupils are competent in these skills before learning the turns.

Grab Turn

In this method the swimmer approaches the wall on the back and the foremost hand 'grabs' the rail or scum trough (fig. 11·37(a)). The body then turns on its side as the arm pulls it close into the wall. The head lifts, the body remains straight whilst the knees are tucked to the chest shortening the lever and therefore increasing the speed of the turn. The body is now turned around to face the wall, with the trailing arm having pushed downward and backward to assist rotation (fig. 11·37(b)). The feet are placed on the wall and the body is allowed to drop back in the

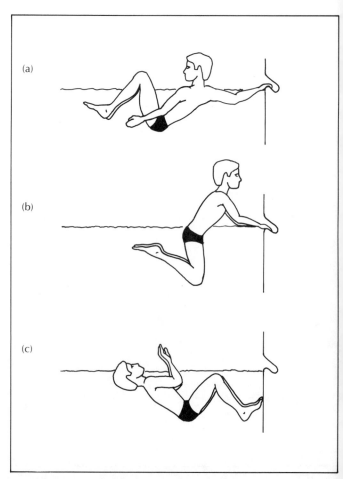

Fig. 11·37

water ready for the extended body glide as previously described for the start (fig. 11·37(c)).

Teaching stages:

1) Hold the rail or trough with one hand whilst lying on the back, lift the head, bend the knees to the chest and turn the body sideways to the wall, toward the touching hand, and pull the body toward the wall.

2) When in the upright position turn the body to face the wall.

3) Place the feet on the wall, move the hands close to the sides of the head, and allow the body to drop backward into the water ready for the push off and extended body glide.

4) Repeat these actions aiming for continuity.

Spin Turn

In the approach, the touching hand will press hard against the wall at or below the water line (fig. 11·38(a)). The head is lifted and at the same time the knees are brought up to the chest (fig. 11·38(b)). The trailing arm will scull to assist the body to spin around toward the wall in the direction of the touching arm (fig. 11·38(c)). The feet are placed on the wall, and the body is dropped backward into the water in preparation for the push off into the extended body glide (fig. 11·38(d)).

Teaching stages:

1) Swim Back Stroke and at a short distance from the wall, lift the head, tuck the knees to the chest and spin the body around. Start the action as one hand is about to enter the water and the opposite arm has finished the propulsion phase.

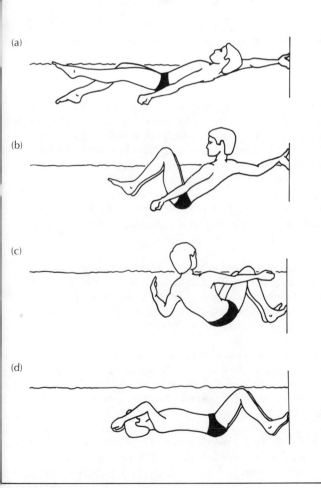

Fig. 11·38

2) Part practice with one arm extended beyond the head and sculling with the other – stress the spin.

3) Repeat the practice sufficiently close to place the feet on the wall when the spin is complete, and follow with a strong push off.

4) Practise the complete turn, aiming for continuity.

The Tumble Turn

This is the fastest Back Stroke Turn and, therefore, the most commonly used in competition.

If possible, the approach (fig. 11·39(a)) is made with the preferred hand touching the wall 0.3/0.6m (12-14ins) below the surface with fingers pointing downward (fig. 11·39(b)). The

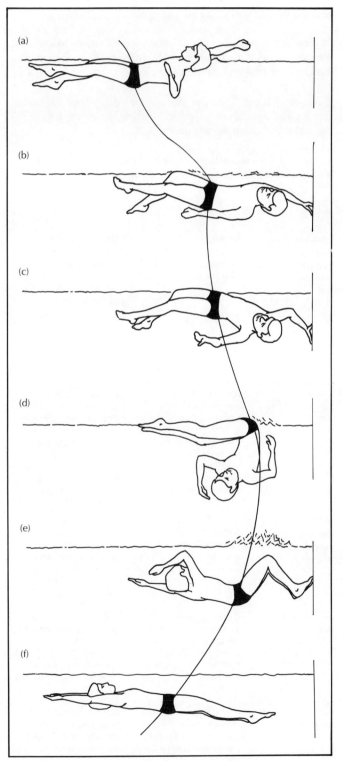

Fig. 11·39

opposite hand having completed its pushing action, assists a backward rotation of the body with a sculling action (fig. 11·39(c)). The touching arm bends as the legs remain on the surface and the body begins to pike. When the hips are over the head which always leads the body (fig. 11·39(d)), the bent touching arm has pushed the body away from the wall and then it joins the sculling hand close to the head. At the same time the legs are swung over the water and dropped so that the feet can be placed on the wall below the surface (fig. 11·39(e)), at a comfortable distance apart, ready for the push off. This must be performed on the back to comply with ASA Law (fig. 11·39(f)).

Teaching stages:

1) Approach the wall as for the spin turn and make the touch 0.3 to 0.6 metres (12-14ins) below the surface. This will necessitate the head going under the water.

2) Repeat this practice until the touch is consistently made with the same hand at the same depth. N.B. The body must remain on the back until the touch has been made.

3) Repeat practice (2) and as the touch is made, move the body into a piked position with the head leading, swing the legs over the water and place the feet on the wall.

4) Attempt the complete action with stress on the push off and glide, in a streamlined position.

Breast Stroke and Butterfly Turns

The approach to the wall, the mechanics of turning and the push off are similar for both strokes, the difference being in the underwater swimming phase.

The present law for turning is the same for both strokes in that it requires the touch to be made with both hands, simultaneously, with the shoulders in the horizontal position. The touch may be at, above or below the water level. For Breast Stroke an uneven touch is permitted but for Butterfly Stroke hands must be on the same level.

The approach to the wall is made without slackening the swimming speed, the arms are extended and the touch is made with both hands to conform with ASA law as previously described. Adjustment to the timing of the final stroke may be required depending upon the approach position of the body, relative to the wall. The swimmer may have to decide whether to stretch for the wall with arms extended and kicking hard to maintain the momentum, or to take another half stroke before touching. There is little difficulty in the Breast Stroke approach for the arm action can be easily modified. The Butterfly approach can cause problems because the the law demands that the arm recovery is made over the water. If the touch on the wall is not likely to coincide with the arm entry and there is doubt if another 'full' arm stroke can be completed in time, it is better if the arms are kept fully extended and forward momentum maintained from the leg drive (fig. 11·40).

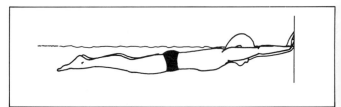

Fig. 11·40

Faults	Causes	Corrections
1) Starting to turn when too far away from the wall	i) Poor judgment; ii) Fear of colliding with the wall.	Repeated practice of the approach using a marker to help identify position of body relative to the wall.
2) Starting to turn too late with the body too close to the wall	Faulty judgement	As above.
3) Pushing off (i) too near the surface; (ii) too deeply	Poor transition from the approach to the turn due to (i) lack of understanding of the action; (ii) not allowing the head to submerge; (iii) poor timing; (iv) trying to avoid discomfort from water entering the nose.	Watch a good demonstration and attempt to copy. Practise the approach with a 'deep' touch. Push and glide practices exhaling slowly through the nose. Push and glide practices stressing the angle of approach to the surface.
4) Pausing after the touch – no continuity of movement	Lack of confidence and/or inability to coordinate the actions required.	i) Repeat demonstration; (ii) Practise with slow approach and stress touch and turn; (iii) repeat the actions aiming for continuity.
5) Pushing off (i) with one foot; (ii) with one or both hands at the side of the body	i) Lack of body awareness and arm positions; (ii) Lack of effort in reaching for stretched streamlined position.	i) Repeat practice of dropping back into the water from the rail; (ii) push-and-glide practice, stressing the push from both feet and stretching the arms.
6) Push off with no glide	i) Incorrect positioning of body for an effective push off; (ii) Failure to use momentum of the push in anxiety to start the swimming action.	Repeat practices to adjust body position at the wall. Repeat with emphasis on a powerful push.

As the touch is made, the elbows flex, the head and shoulders lift, as the knees are bent. The head rotates to the preferred side as the arm on that side is pulled back with the elbow bent (fig. 11·41(a)). The other arm assists the turn by pushing the body away from the wall (fig. 11·41(b)). As this pushing arm moves to join the free arm the knees are bent and the feet are planted firmly on the wall (fig. 11·41(c)). The head drops beneath the surface as the arms begin to extend (fig. 11·41(d)). With head down, the legs thrust the body vigorously from the wall in a streamlined position (fig. 11·41(e)).

The depth of the push off and the underwater swimming action is shallower in Butterfly than in Breast Stroke. The law appertaining to both strokes states that the body must be perfectly on the breast as the feet leave the wall. However, following this, the law differs for each stroke.

In Butterfly the law allows for as many leg kicks as the swimmer wishes to make, but it allows only one arm pull. The recovery has to wait until part of the body has reached the surface, because the recovery must take place over the surface of the water.

In Breast Stroke the law permits one complete stroke cycle before surfacing. In order to take full advantage of this the push off may be deeper than that for Butterfly. It must be noted that a second stroke cycle may not be started until the head has broken the surface.

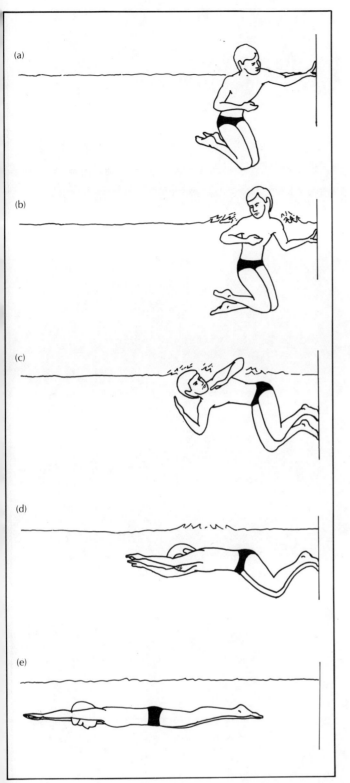

(a)

(b)

(c)

(d)

(e)

Fig. 11·41

4) Repeat practices with particular attention to the following points:

a) placing the feet against the wall at the correct height and distance apart,

b) turning the head quickly to the preferred side whilst releasing the hand on that same side,

c) assisting the swing of the feet and the turn with a vigorous push with the arm on the opposite side from the turn,

d) having released both arms in the turn, practise dropping in the water with a half twist, to ensure that the body will be 'perfectly on the breast' when the push from the wall is made.

5) Practise the push and glide underwater at the depth suited to the swimmer/and for the stroke being performed.

6) Practise the co-ordination of all the actions with emphasis on the following points:

a) for Breast Stroke – modified arm pull to the sides, the arm and leg recovery, the leg kick into the second glide phase and surfacing,

b) for Butterfly – one arm pull followed by the appropriate number of leg kicks required to maintain underwater momentum and to bring the body to the surface for the recovery of the arms, for the start of the swim cycle.

Teaching Stages

1) Practise kicking towards the wall with arms extended forward for the hands to touch at or near water level.

2) Swim full stroke at 'racing' speed learning to adjust the action for the touch to be made with arms extended. NB: In the Butterfly stroke the recovery must always be made over the water and not through the water as in the Breast Stroke.

3) Repeat 2) practising lifting the head and shoulders and bending the knees to assist the body swing into a near vertical position.

Reader's notes

Chapter 12

Survival in Water

Any comprehensive programme of swimming in a club or school should include activities which develop water confidence and cover the principles of survival in an emergency.

The manner in which a swimmer would apply training would be determined by the nature of the emergency but competence in swimming would always be an advantage. Therefore, a variety of strokes should be learned to prepare for all possible situations.

In recent years there has been a considerable amount of research in the subject of survival in cold water and it has been firmly established that where the casualty is at some distance from safety, the most important consideration must be the conservation of body heat, by avoiding unnecessary exertion and retaining clothing. It is important to have a clear interpretation of any situation where this principle must be applied. Anyone slipping off the edge of a canal or riverbank is within a few feet of land and in the vast majority of cases could swim the short distance to safety. However, if an accident were to occur at a fair distance from land, the person would need to make some crucial decisions which would be influenced by swimming ability, the water temperature, floatation support available and clothing being worn. This emphasises the need for swimmers, particularly young children, to be educated in all aspects of survival.

When the water temperature is below 25°C (around the British Isles it rarely reaches 15°C) any movement carried out by human beings in the water will lead to a drop in body temperature because exercise increases the blood flow to the body surfaces. The heat in this blood is then removed by the cold water and the cooled blood is subsequently left to complete its circulation through the body. Movement of the limbs causes the water trapped between garments and the body surfaces to be displaced and, subsequently, replaced by colder water, thus diminishing the insulating effect of the clothing. As these processes continue, a gradual reduction in the core temperature of the body takes place.

Prevention of emergencies

Many emergencies arise because recommended safety practices have not been followed. Any programme of survival training should include the principles of safety for water activities. The common features of all codes of practice for activities involving a water environment may be summarised as follows:

DO NOT swim alone unless competent help is at hand.
DO NOT bathe in areas where red flags or other warnings are displayed.
DO NOT fool about at the sides of rivers, lakes, canals or quay sides.
DO NOT venture on frozen ponds without making sure that they are safe.
DO NOT float out to sea on air beds even if you are a strong swimmer for tides can be treacherous.
DO NOT go out in small boats without wearing a life jacket.

Fig. 12·1

Fig. 12·2

In emergency situations involving upturned boats the casualty should, if possible, stay with the boat and in some circumstances preserve heat by climbing out of the water on to the upturned hull (figs. 12·1, 12·2).

SURVIVAL SKILLS

Entering the water

In most situations where survival techniques are required, those involved will not be making deliberate entries into the water. On the contrary, they should be concerned with staying out of it.

However, in some situations where, perhaps, a vessel maybe sinking or burning it may be necessary to enter the water voluntarily. The safest method is to slide in or to clamber down a rope thus avoiding the danger of collision with floating debris or underwater objects. Where it is not possible to slide into the water, the entry should be made from the lowest possible height, by jumping using the 'bomb' or 'tuck jump'.

This entry requires the person to step away from the starting point and then to draw up the knees to the chest until the seat and feet are approximately at the same level. This should ensure that the seat and feet are the first parts of the body to make contact with the water. It may be found advantageous to wrap the hands and arms around the legs in order to hold the position more securely (fig. 12·3).

Fig. 12·3

From heights of approximately one metre, the 'scissor' jump might be used. This involves a single foot take off from the starting point. It is more accurately described as a 'step off' rather than a jump. By entering the water with one leg forward and the other leg backward and with the arms stretched forward sideways at about shoulder level, the area which makes impact with the water is increased and the depth of immersion is kept to a minimum (fig. 12·4).

Fig. 12·4

Treading Water

Most emergencies in which survival techniques are required take place within sight of land therefore, the first reaction of the casualty should be to attract the attention of others. This can be done by gently treading water whilst waving with one or both hands. If more than one person is involved in the emergency, efforts to attract attention should be organised, to avoid having too many individuals signalling at the same time, thereby wasting energy. As part of the energy conservation process, all clothing except heavy outer garments and footwear should be retained. Saturated coats and footwear filled with water will act as weights and cause the casualty to sink or expend vital energy in overcoming the additional downward drag.

The prime aim of treading water should be to keep the swimmer in one place, in an upright position with the head above water,

the actions of the limbs requiring no more effort than that required to prevent sinking.

In order to minimise the expenditure of energy and the movement of water between body and clothing, gentle movements of the legs should be used, such as;

a) a slow, steady breaststroke type action,

b) a cycling action, with legs bending alternately beneath the body, or

c) a flutter kick, similar to the alternating crawl kick.

The arms assist the leg action and help to provide stability by pressing against the water, with the hands performing sculling actions.

In all actions the force is directed downwards to produce an upward reaction (fig. 12·5).

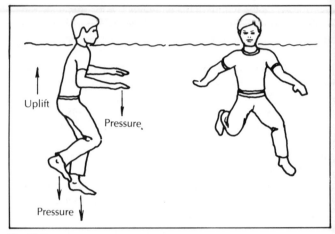

Fig. 12·5

When learning the skill, pupils can practise within their own standing depth of water. In the initial stages floats might be used until they discover, by trial, the most effective leg action. Competent swimmers will easily relate leg actions to those of the strokes and merely modify them for application in the vertical position. In deep water, the less able pupils should stay near the pool-side whilst practising. Once the skill has been established it can be developed by using one or various actions for timed periods. Limb injuries can be simulated by immobilising one or more of them and stronger kicks can be encouraged by reaching upward with the arms.

Sculling

In survival situations, sculling is used mainly to accompany the leg action in supporting the body in an upright position, the arms and hands remaining approximately at chest level in the water.

Detailed descriptions of sculling actions are given in Chapter 13. Adaptations of these may be required in survival situations.

Heat Escape Lessening Posture (HELP)

This is alternatively known as "Heat Expending Lessening Posture" since not only must heat be conserved but no more energy than is absolutely necessary must be expended in attempts to remain afloat.

The posture is most easily and effectively achieved when a good quality life jacket is being worn (fig. 12·6). Nevertheless the HELP position can be adapted and adopted wherever floating objects are available (fig. 12·7).

The principle involved is that those parts of the body which lose heat most easily should be protected as effectively as possible, whilst keeping the head out of water. The lower limbs should be pressed together tightly with the knees bent and the upper legs drawn up to cover as much of the abdomen as possible and thereby, reducing heat loss from the groin. The upper arms should be held close to the sides of the body with the forearms held close alongside the bent legs (fig. 12·6). Some people may find the position easier with the lower legs crossed over. The shape adopted by the body should be similar to that of the squat position.

The angle of tilt of the body in the HELP position will be determined, largely, by the nature and positioning of any float support in use.

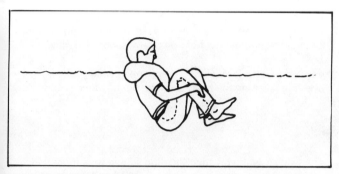

Fig. 12·6 HELP with life jacket

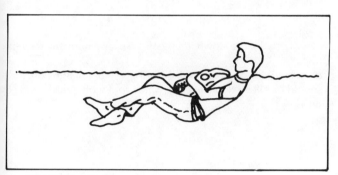

Fig. 12·7 HELP with float material

The Huddle

Where several people are involved, simultaneously, in an emergency they may assist each other in conserving heat by huddling together as closely as possible. The effectiveness of the huddle will depend upon the type of float support available. Where all of those involved are wearing life jackets, the most effective formation is probably that of a tightly held circle (fig. 12·8).

Floating objects such as a lifebelt or large block of timber could be used for support, always remembering that the abdomen and

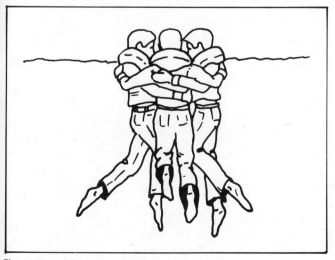

Fig. 12·8 Huddle with life jackets

sides of the chest should be protected as much as possible, to reduce heat loss to a minimum. Signalling for help should be performed, in turn, by each person (fig. 12·9).

Fig. 12·9 'Huddle' with float material

Climbing Out

A number of emergency situations occur in canals locks and harbours where the water level can be some distance below the edge of the parapet. It is, therefore, useful for swimmers to learn to be proficient in climbing out of the water in such circumstances. A knowledge of techniques suited to walls, ropes and rope ladders is invaluable and if suitable equipment is available practice can take place in the environment of the swimming pool.

Without steps or handhold and if the parapet is not too high, a competent swimmer may be able to kick vigorously to rise out of the water high enough to grasp the edge with finger tips, then to heave himself up until the arms are extended vertically downward and supporting the body. Some swimmers may need to perform the lifting action with a few short pulls increasing the displacement of water on each repetition. From this position supported on the arms, the upper body can be bent forward to enable one leg to be raised sideways to place the foot on the parapet before scrambling over the top to safety.

Fig. 12·10

Teaching and Organisation

Many of the skills used in Survival Swimming will be learned as part of a normal swimming programme. The first requirement is the ability to keep oneself afloat and to move about in the water with the minimum expenditure of energy. Progress is made by learning and using various strokes, and swimming for longer distances. Other skills such as treading water, practising HELP and Huddle positions and sculling will also be learned.

During an orthodox lesson with a class of mixed ability some of the survival skills might be learned and practised by one group, while other groups may be learning basic skills or developing stroke techniques.

A time-distance lesson might include survival practices for one or more groups e.g. swimming for distance, without touching the pool-side for a set time, with changes of stroke at set intervals. Other challenges may be included, in accordance with the ability of swimmers.

Occasionally, a whole lesson might be devoted to survival swimming, some skills being taught as a class activity, across the pool or in free formation, other skills being taught and practised with the class arranged in groups.

Before attempting an intensive programme of survival swimming, pupils should be competent in a variety of strokes and able to swim a distance of at least 400 metres.

In the early stages, skills may be practised in swimwear and later in clothing. When the skills have been learned, a series of realistic situations can be simulated to add interest and motivation. Finally, survival swimming could culminate in the preparation and tests for ASA Survival Awards at appropriate levels.

Hypothermia
It should be realised that survival practices in the safety and warmth of a swimming pool are far different from the discomforts likely to be encountered in a real life situation.

While it is possible to learn and to practise skills, which can be related to situations of survival in open water, no one would suggest, for obvious reasons, that first-hand experience which might lead to Hypothermia, should be part of the training. However, it is essential that the dangers of exposure and causes of Hypothermia should be made known to those who practise 'Survival Swimming' so that appropriate prevention action could be taken should they find themselves in the real situation.

At all times, the teacher concerned with training should be watchful for symptoms of exposure, particularly if working in outdoor pool, lake, river, or sea. Even indoors, water temperatures could fall to a level in which exercise produces a cooling effect on the body (i.e. less than 25°C, 77°F).

There are many situations in which people can be subjected to exposure but the one with which we are immediately concerned is immersion in cold water. The severe chilling of the body surface leading to a progressive fall in body temperature could lead to death from Hypothermia.

The progressive symptoms are;
a) shivering, which is a natural compensatory method of heat production,
b) persistent muscular rigidity,
c) unconsciousness.

Factors leading to heat loss are;
a) lack of the subcutaneous fat, which forms an insulating layer,
b) lack of suitable clothing which tends to maintain a warm layer of air between its inner surface and the skin,
c) low water temperature causing heat to be conducted from the person,

d) physical exertion increasing blood flow to outer parts of the body where it is more easily cooled,
e) movement in the water, causing the loss of a warm layer of air allowing cold water to circulate between body and clothing.

A swimmer in the real situation should be aware of the fact that the increased weight of clothing can impede and cause fatigue. Heavy woollen garments and those with wide mesh are rarely of value and these should be removed and discarded at the first sign of their becoming waterlogged. It should be remembered, however, that in very cold water clothing can act as an insulator preventing loss of body heat.

Having given careful consideration to these factors the swimmer should,
a) consider how much clothing should be retained,
b) avoid excessive movement in keeping afloat until rescued,
c) avoid swimming but hold on to any supportive material if possible,
d) if no support is available, simply tread water, as gently as possible, keeping the head and face out of water.

The teacher in the practice situation should remember that;
a) children are more susceptible to chilling effects than has been generally accepted,
b) children (being generally thinner) cool more rapidly than adults,
c) girls cool more slowly than boys, because normally they have more fat,
d) a child, looking cold and shivering, or complaining of cold, should be allowed to leave the water, to dry off quickly and get dressed.

Chapter 13

Recreative Swimming

In addition to the four strokes already described there are others not used, nowadays, in competition. Nevertheless they are well worth learning for recreational purposes or for their adaptation and application to other activities in water.

Elementary Back Stroke

Body Position

The body lies on the back in an almost horizontal position with the face clear of the water. With the head raised a little or with the eyes looking towards the feet, a lower leg position will result, so that the knees are not likely to break the water surface on recovery. The increased resistance caused by this position presents no problem because speed is unimportant.

Leg Action

The purpose of the leg kick is to provide propulsion and to maintain the desired body position. The pathway of the action is similar to that of an 'inverted Breast Stroke', and the emphasis should be on flexed ankles so that the kick is felt to be made with the soles of the feet.

a) **Recovery** In this action the knees are bent by dropping the lower legs with heels moving towards the seat. The heels should be hip width or more apart, ready for the drive backwards. The thighs remain almost in line with the body just under the surface of the water. The position of the knees is relatively unimportant although the distance between tends to be narrow rather than wide. A wide action of the feet will cause some flexion of the hips and the body to be more inclined to the surface.

b) **Propulsion** With the heels well apart and the ankles flexed, the drive is slightly outward and backward. The feet move through a circular pathway and the inside borders, as well as the sides of the feet, push against the water to gain propulsion. The legs may or may not move together depending on the activity for which the stroke is intended.

Arm Action

This might be described as a wide sculling action.

a) **Recovery** The hands are moved simultaneously under water, being pulled upward, close to the body, from thighs to chest, then swept sideways until the arms are extended and almost in line with the shoulders, in preparation for the propulsive action.

b) **Propulsion** With the palms of the hands gaining purchase on the water, the extended arms are pressed strongly inwards, towards the sides of the body.

Breathing

No problems are presented because the face is clear of the water throughout the stroke. Normally, breath would be taken on recovery and exhaled with propulsion.

Co-ordination

This is fairly simple. Leg movements tend to precede arm actions but they appear to be simultaneous. There is no pause between the end of recovery and the beginning of propulsion. A glide may be held with the body in an extended position, at the end of the propulsive actions.

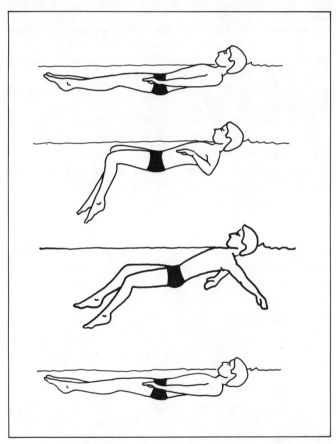

Fig. 13·1   Elementary Back Stroke Sequence

Variations

a) With small sculling actions with the hands remaining at the sides of the body.

b) Without the use of hands, by placing them on the hips.

c) With the hands, over the chest, in a position which could support a person for towing. In this situation a continuous kicking action would be required with the legs not coming together after the propulsive movement.

English Back Stroke

This is a development of the Elementary Back Stroke performed with an identical leg action, already described, but using a double over arm action.

Arm Action

a) **Recovery** From a position at the sides of the body the arms are lifted from the water, simultaneously, and then carried to an extended position in advance of the head. They enter the water, slightly wider than the shoulders, dependent mainly on the flexibility of the shoulder girdle. When the hands are about six inches below the surface the pull begins after a smooth transition from the entry.

b) **Propulsion** With the arms remaining straight, the hands follow semi-circular pathways. They are at their deepest in the water as they pass the shoulders when the pull changes to a push. This continues until the hands reach the hips, with the arms at the sides of the body.

Breathing

Normally, inhalation takes place as the arms swing overhead, during which action there is a slight raising of the head and upper body. Exhalation takes place during propulsion.

Timing

The recovery of the arms, coincides with the propulsive action of the legs, at the end of which movement, the body is fully extended with the arms overhead. The legs remain close together during the powerful pull-push action of the arms.

Variations

1) Timing can be modified to allow a long glide;

a) When the body is extended with the arms overhead, at the end of the propulsive action of the legs, or

b) When the arms are at the sides of the body at the end of their propulsive action.

2) A bent arm action may be used.

As the arms pull, the elbows bend and when the hands reach the line of the shoulders they are in position to allow a powerful push, which continues until the arms are extended by the sides of the body. This variation can be used when learning to perform a bent arm pull for the Back Crawl stroke.

Side Stroke

As the name suggests, the swimmer lies in the water, on either side, as streamlined and horizontal as possible. The side of the head is in the water with the eyes and nose just above the surface.

Leg Action

From an extended position and moving simultaneously, the legs with one above the other, begin their recovery. The upper leg moves forward and the lower leg moves backward with the knees bending and the heels moving towards the seat. Propulsion occurs as the legs are swept together through a circular pathway, back to the extended position which is held during a glide. The action is sometimes called a 'scissor' kick.

Arm Action

During the glide, the upper arm lies along the upper side of the body with the lower arm extended forward in advance of the head. From these positions the arms move simultaneously. The upper arm recovers as it moves forward to a position with elbow bent and the hand below the head. At the same time the lower arm is propelling as it pulls in a downward-sideways direction to meet the other arm in a similar position, with elbow bent and the hand below the head. Still moving simultaneously and without

pausing the arms are now extended with the upper arm propelling as it pushes downward-backward, while the lower arm recovers, as it extends to the forward position.

Breathing

Inhalation normally takes place during the propulsive action of the lower arm which tends to raise the upper body and head and as the glide begins, exhalation takes place through nose and mouth.

Co-ordination

From the extended position, while the arms are moving inward to their bent positions, the legs recover to their bent positions ready for the propulsive kick, which is accompanied by the extension of the arms. Then follows a short glide before the actions are repeated.

Variations

This stroke may also be performed as follows;

a) with an out of water recovery of the upper arm using an action similar to that of the Front Crawl Stroke,

b) with each arm recovering over the water with the body rolling alternately to the side of the pulling arm, and with each leg in turn being uppermost during the kick. It was from this latter form that the Front Crawl stroke was originally developed.

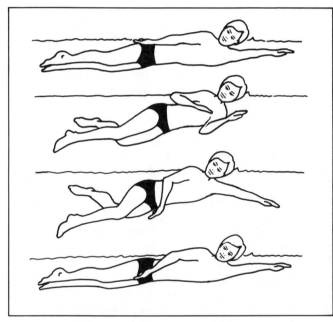

Fig. 13·2 Side Stroke Sequence

Front Paddle

The swimmer is in a prone and horizontal position. The leg action is similar to that of Front Crawl. The alternate action of the arms takes place entirely underwater by pulling downwards and backward from a forward position and recovering close to the surface. The length of the arm action may vary from a short one in advance of the shoulders to a longer one, with the arms fully extended in front and pulling back to a position determined by the need for a smooth transition to recovery.

Miscellaneous Skills

By exploiting the principles of buoyancy, balance and movement in water, there can be a wide variety of comparatively easy skills which will provide interesting and enjoyable challenges to the swimmer.

One of the fundamental actions featuring prominently in the performance of many aspects of watermanship is sculling and the early mastery of this action is strongly recommended.

Fig. 13·3   Front Paddle

Sculling

Stationary Scull on the Back

The swimmer adopts a flat position on the back with the arms straight and by the sides of the body. As the hands move away from the body the leading edges (little fingers) of the hands are raised so that the palms are facing outwards and downwards. On the inward movement the leading edges (thumbs) are again raised so that the palms are facing inwards and downwards at the extremity of each inward and outward sweep, the hands rotate to change the angle of the palms. The arms should be straight and held without undue tension with the movement initiated at the shoulders and passing through the elbows, wrists and hands and not confined to the lower arms. It is essential that throughout the scull the wrists remain in line with the forearms and that the arms should remain close to the body. The downward pressure of the palms has an upward reaction which counteracts the tendency of the body to sink, providing the necessary support to allow it to remain stationary at the water surface (fig. 13·4).

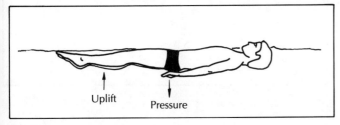

Fig. 13·4

Head First Scull on the Back

The swimmer adopts a flat position on the back with the arms straight and by the sides of the body. The wrists are bent backwards so that the fingers are tipped upward with palms facing towards the feet. The basic sculling action as described for the stationary scull is then performed. The body, fully extended, should remain flat, with the face, hips, knees and toes at the surface (fig. 13·5).

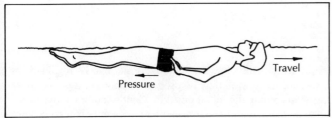

Fig. 13·5

Feet First Scull on the Back

The swimmer adopts a flat position on the back with the arms straight and by the sides of the body. The wrists are flexed (bent forwards) so that the fingers are facing towards the bottom of the pool, palms facing towards the head. The same basic sculling action, is performed, as described opposite. A circular 'Breast Stroke type action' will provide propulsion, but it should not be encouraged if progress to advanced skills is anticipated (figs. 13·6, 13·7).

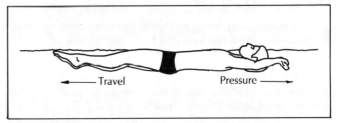

Fig. 13·6

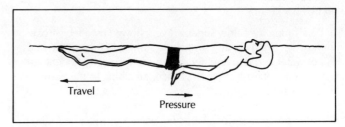

Fig. 13·7

In devising water skills in general, consideration should be given to the following basic aspects relating to watermanship:

a) Learning to balance in the water with the body taking different shapes – wide, tucked, elongated, symmetrical and asymmetrical.

b) Travelling in various directions, forwards, backwards, sideways.

c) Turning, rotating and spinning through various axes with the body elongated, tucked, in prone and supine positions (fig. 13·8).

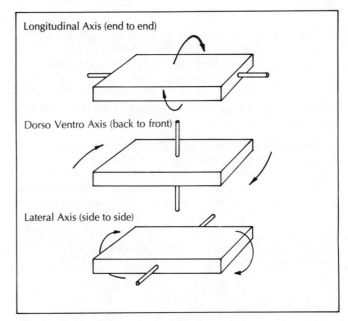

Fig. 13·8

d) Game like activities, using rings, hoops, or playballs; working with partners: simple 2 v 2 games and easily organised races.

The following examples indicate, more specifically, some forms which might be attempted:

a) In prone or supine position, attempting to float with limbs in different positions, e.g. legs together arms overhead; body and limbs forming a star shape.

b) In supine position, arms at the sides, one leg raised vertically – using sculling actions to propel the body head first, submerging and rising to the surface during travel.

c) In supine position, knees and lower legs raised towards chest at water level – sculling to spin the body in clockwise or anti-clockwise directions.

d) In similar position to c) with body tilted sideways – sculling action to spin in either direction, at the same time using a scissor kick with feet breaking the water surface.

e) In prone or supine position with body tucked – rotating forwards or backwards to perform somersaults.

Similar rotations may be performed with the body piked or arched backwards.

f) Performing a shallow surface dive followed by a few strokes underwater, then kicking strongly to surface to project the body out of water and into another shallow surface dive. Repeat the actions continuously over a distance, breathing as the body moves over the water.

Detailed descriptions of a variety of water skills will be found in the ASA publication 'Teaching Synchronised Swimming'.

Floating

In order to conserve energy or to rest, the swimmer might have recourse to floating with little or no movement and this can be achieved in various ways:

a) **Mushroom Float** Adopting a prone and tucked position with chin held towards the chest, knees towards the head, arms held loosely around lower legs and lungs inflated, the swimmer will float with the rounded back out of water. The general appearance is similar to the head of a mushroom (fig. 13·9). The skill may be first practised in shallow water, where, not only is the position easy to assume, but it is also easy for the swimmer to regain a standing position.

b) **Prone Float** In this method, the legs are extended, the arms are in a comfortable forward position, the head is down with the face in the water. From this position it is easy to make body adjustments which will allow breathing to take place and for progress to be made if required. This skill may first be learned and practised in shallow water by taking a breath and leaning gently forward (fig. 13·10).

c) **Vertical Float** With arms relaxed below the surface, a position is adopted best suited for gaining and preserving balance. The head is held backward with the nose and mouth just above the water surface. The skill may be practised in water of just more than shoulder depth, making necessary adjustments until the full support of the water is felt. Optimum buoyancy is achieved by allowing the body to assume a natural submerged position in the water and maintaining a constant supply of air in the lungs (fig. 13·11).

d) **Supine Float** This method allows the face to be maintained clear of the water but it is probably the most difficult to accomplish, requiring fine balance and delicate limb adjustments. The skill should be first practised in water of a

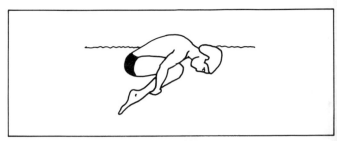

Fig. 13·9

Fig. 13·10

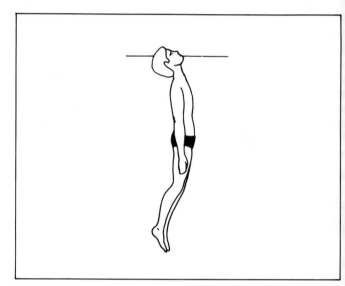

Fig. 13·11

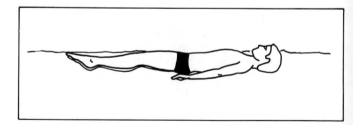

Fig. 13·12

depth which will allow the standing position to be regained easily. The pool rail or wall may be used for support, or a partner may assist in gaining the initial position. Gentle sculling movements may be made with the hands until a buoyant, balanced position is achieved and the upthrust of the water experienced (fig. 13·12).

Surface Diving

There are two methods of surface diving of which the head first dive is well known, but equally effective and easier to perform is that of submerging feet first.

For the head first dive, the Swimmer, moving in a prone position, performs a strong Breast Stroke arm pull which is continued towards the sides of the body. During the pull the head and shoulders are thrust forcibly downward whilst the body bends sharply at the hips. As the body now rotates the arms are swept forward underwater, the reaction of which enables the legs to be raised upward to a vertical position. The whole body now in line, submerges under its own weight. It is important that the swimmer should have the confidence and ability to remain in the vertical position for some time, to allow the weight of the legs to assist the descent. As the dive requires the body to be rotated until it is inverted, skills such as hand standing in shallow water and somersaulting are useful preparatory activities which will also help to establish confidence agility and control of breathing (fig. 13·13).

The feet first dive has the disadvantage that the body position has to be adjusted in order to begin swimming underwater. The dive is performed by making a powerful downward Breast Stroke type kick together with a vigorous downward thrust with the hands, thus raising the upper part of the body as high as possible from the water. With maximum body weight above the surface, with the legs brought together and the arms held at the sides, the streamlined body will sink below the surface. At the end of the dive, the body can be tucked and brought into a horizontal position from which underwater swimming can begin with an action similar to that of Breast Stroke recovery (fig. 13·14). If greater depth is required before swimming begins, the hands can be pressed upwards towards the surface, so forcing the body deeper in the water.

Alternatively, in performing the dive, the arms can be raised above the head following the leg kick, thereby adding to the unsupported weight of the upper body and assisting the sinking process. This method has advantages for swimmers with a weak kick who find difficulty in forcing the upper part of the body above the water surface. However, it has the disadvantage that it makes the transfer to the swimming position more difficult to achieve.

Fig. 13·13

Fig. 13·14

Underwater Swimming

After the surface dive, the logical progression is the underwater swim. Methods of achieving propulsion are:

a) Using a Breast Stroke leg action with the arms pulling around to the sides of the body.

b) Using the same arm action with a crawl type kick.

c) Using a front paddle action with the arms and a crawl type kick.

Chapter 14

Resuscitation

[Adapted and abridged, with permission, from 'Resuscitation and First Aid' 5th Edition 1986, published by The Royal Life Saving Society U.K.]

Resuscitation is the act of reviving a nearly-dead or apparently dead person. It is necessary if breathing is inadequate or the heart has stopped beating (cardiac arrest). The brain is the most sensitive part of the body; within seconds of the heart stopping consciousness will be lost, and within a few minutes death will occur. Resuscitation must be started as soon as possible. The stages are:

● Ensuring an adequate airway
● Artificial ventilation by the Expired Air method
● Restoration of the circulation by External Chest Compression.
As an aid to memory this can be thought of as:
  A = Airway
  B = Breathing
  C = Circulation

Expired Air Resuscitation

Expired Air Resuscitation (EAR), sometimes known as the "kiss of life", has been shown to be much more effective than any other technique of artificial ventilation that does not rely on special equipment. Basically, it consists of the rescuer blowing air into a casualty's lungs by applying his own mouth to the casualty's mouth or nose. Although the air which the rescuer breathes out only contains 16 per cent oxygen compared with 21 per cent in the atmosphere, this is quite enough to keep the casualty alive.

Even if the casualty is in fact still breathing, EAR is harmless. Indeed, if respirations are weak they can be greatly helped by EAR applied at the same time.

The method can be taught easily to all age groups but its one main drawback is that it can be unpleasant for the rescuer. Casualties, particularly from drowning, often vomit and this may necessitate a change from mouth-to-mouth to mouth-to-nose resuscitation. The two methods have been shown to be equally effective in achieving ventilation.

External Chest Compression

External Chest Compression (ECC) will maintain circulation of the blood when the heart has stopped, and it may stimulate it into beating again. It consists of rhythmical compressions of the casualty's chest, achieved by the rescuer pressing down with his hand on the sternum (breast bone). There is some risk of damage to the heart, chest wall and abdominal organs during ECC. This risk is far outweighed by its lifesaving potential, but it does mean that it is vital to be sure of the diagnosis of cardiac arrest before starting.

It is important to remember that ECC and EAR, even when applied skilfully, may not result in the casualty's recovery if too much damage has occurred to the heart or there has been a delay before resuscitation has been started. Provided that the rescuer has applied the techniques in a correct and careful manner he should have no cause for self-criticism whatever the outcome.

Sequence of Resuscitation

1. Check Whether Casualty is Conscious

Gently shake his shoulders and say loudly "Are you awake? Can you hear me?"

● If he responds by answering or moving, check that his breathing is normal (see below). If so, leave him in the position in which you find him (provided he is not in further danger) and check for any injury before trying to move him.

● If he is unconscious or you are not sure that his breathing is normal . . .

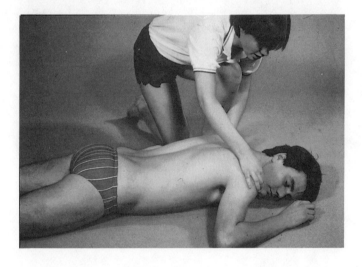

2. Check Whether Casualty is Breathing

Look for movement of the chest.

Feel and listen at the mouth for breathing, which should be quiet – a wheeze or rattle indicates obstruction.

Look for cyanosis – this is a bluish discoloration of the face, ears and nails which shows that the blood contains very little oxygen.

● If he is breathing quietly, place him in the Recovery Position (see overleaf) unless this would aggravate an injury.

● Keep him under close observation and keep checking that he is breathing freely.

● If he is not breathing, if breathing is obstructed or if in any doubt . . .

3. Turn Casualty Onto His Back

It is important to turn the casualty over as quickly as possible whilst exercising great care, particularly not to injure his head.

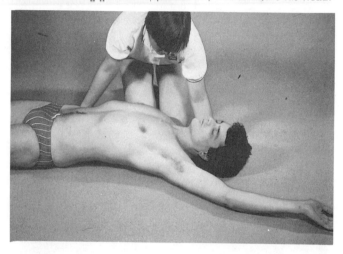

4. Obtain a Clear Airway

With the casualty on his back, quickly remove any debris or *loose* false teeth from his mouth – leave well-fitting dentures in place.

Loosen tight clothing around his neck.

Lift his chin with the fingers of one hand placed under the bony part of the jaw, near the point of the chin.

At the same time extend his neck by pressing downwards, just above his forehead, with your other hand; this will often allow breathing to restart, or obstructed breathing to improve.

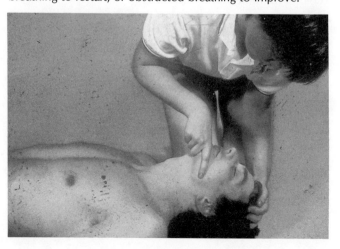

● If breathing does not become normal . . .

5. Start Expired Air Resuscitation

Maintain chin lift and neck extension.

Pinch the soft part of his nose closed with finger and thumb

Allow the casualty's mouth to open a little, but maintain chin lift.

Take a full deep breath and place your lips around his mouth making sure you have a good seal.

Breathe steadily into his mouth, watching from the corner of your eye for his chest to rise.

Maintaining chin lift and neck extension, take your mouth away from the casualty, take another full breath and repeat the sequence as above.

If difficulty is experienced in inflating the chest, change to the mouth-to-nose technique: release his nose and close his mouth. Seal your mouth around his nose and blow steadily as for the mouth-to-mouth technique.

● If breathing does not restart during or immediately after the two initial breaths of EAR . . .

6. Check Casualty's Pulse

The best pulse to feel in an emergency is the carotid, which is found in the neck.

Ensure that the casualty's neck is extended.

Feel for the "Adams Apple" - a hard piece of cartilage in the midline of the neck about halfway between chin and upper part of the sternum. It is more prominent in men.

Slide two fingers from the "Adam's Apple" sideways until they meet a strap-like muscle. Just beneath this can be felt the pulse.

Feel for five seconds before deciding it is absent.

● If the pulse is present:

Maintain chin lift and neck extension.

repeat breaths of EAR at a rate of one every five seconds, taking about one-and-a-half to two seconds to inflate the casualty's chest.

Watch for the chest to rise and then fall, showing that the inflations are effective.

• If the pulse is absent: assume that cardiac arrest has occurred, provided the casualty is:

– Still unconscious
– Making no movement or shivering
– "Deathly" pale or blue

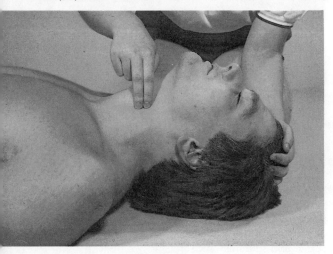

7. Start External Chest Compression

Ensure that the casualty is on a flat, firm surface.

Feel for the lower borders of the rib cage, removing outer clothing if necessary. Identify the lower end of the sternum, which is where the two rib borders meet. Find the notch at the top of the sternum.

From these two landmarks locate the centre of the sternum.

Place the heel of one hand on the centre of the lower half of the sternum, with your other hand on top. Keep your fingers interlocked and raised to ensure that pressure is not applied over the ribs.

With your arms straight, press down vertically on the sternum.

Release the pressure, then repeat at a rate of about one compression a second (60-80 per minute).

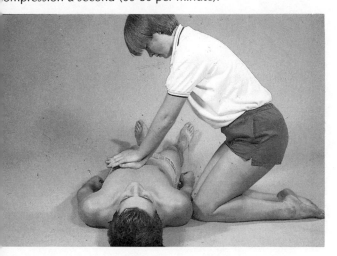

In an unconscious adult you should aim to press down approximately 4-5 centimetres and apply only enough pressure to achieve this. At all times the pressure should be firm, controlled and applied vertically. Try and spend about the same time in the compressed as the released phase.

8. External Chest Compression combined with Expired Air Resuscitation is known as Cardio Pulmonary Resuscitation (CPR)

It is essential to combine EAR with ECC in order that the blood which is being artificially circulated should contain adequate amounts of oxygen.

After 15 compressions of ECC immediately lift the chin and extend the neck.

Give two full breaths of EAR.

Return immediately to ECC without waiting for expiration to occur.

Continue resuscitation by alternating 15 compressions with 2 inflations.

If during combined ECC and EAR the casualty makes a movement or takes a spontaneous breath, check the carotid pulse to see if the heart is beating. Otherwise only interrupt resuscitation after the first minute and then at three minute intervals. Take no more than five seconds to confirm that no pulse is present.

When you are sure that a normal heartbeat has returned and the casualty is breathing on his own without any signs of obstruction you should:

Maintain a good airway and check at frequent intervals that the pulse and respiration remain normal.

Quickly examine the casualty for any injuries; in particular checking for bleeding.

Place him in the Recovery Position.

The Recovery Position

With the casualty on his back, kneel at his side and draw his far arm across his upper chest.

Tuck his nearer hand under his buttock.

Cross his far lower leg over the nearer one.

Take a firm grip of his far hip and shoulder and roll him carefully towards you. Support his head with your other hand to prevent injury.

Allow the weight of his body to rest against your thighs and lower his head carefully to the ground.

Place his upper arm and thigh at right angles to his body. This supports the weight of his chest and abdomen and keeps them clear of the ground, making it easier for him to breathe.

Adjust his lower arm so that it is behind and close to his body.

Keep his airway clear by tilting his head back, holding the jaw forward and mouth open.

Keep the casualty under close observation.

Be prepared to restart resuscitation if necessary.

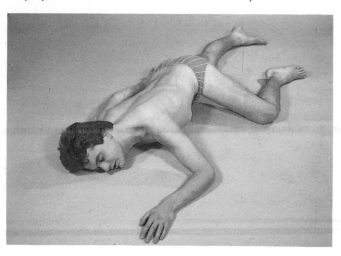

Resuscitation of Babies

When carrying out EAR, apply your mouth over the baby's mouth and nose. In spite of the small size of a baby's lungs the resistance to inflation is about that of an adult. The same effort therefore is needed during EAR, but the amount of air to fill the lungs is much less. Blow in fairly slowly, stopping as soon as you see the chest rise. Increase the rate to 20-25 times a minute.

For ECC, the pressure of two fingers is enough. The compression rate should be 100 per minute, and the depth of compression 1.5-2.5 centimetres.

For both EAR and ECC a baby may be held in your arms. Sufficient support for compression can be given by placing one hand underneath the baby's back.

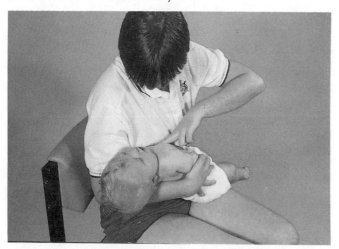

Resuscitation of Children

Whether mouth-to-mouth or mouth-to-mouth-and-nose is used for EAR depends upon the difference in size between you and the child. You will have to make a judgement about this and about the degree of pressure and rate of inflation required.

For children up to about the age of 10 years, ECC should be carried out using one hand only. The rate of compression will depend upon the age and size of the child, varying between about 100 compressions a minute for a baby and the usual adult rate of 60 compressions a minute for a 10-year-old child. The depth of compression should be 2.5-3.5 centimetres.

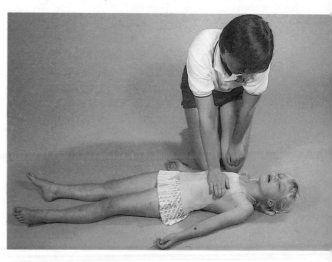

Resuscitation in the Water

ECC cannot be carried out in the water because it is not possible to provide sufficient support behind the casualty's back. EAR is possible whilst swimming in deep water, but this requires a considerable degree of skill, a powerful swimming stroke and stamina. EAR is relatively easy with some sort of support, such as the side of the pool, or whilst standing in shallow water. However, unless you have been fully trained in these techniques it is usually better quickly to tow the non-breathing casualty to the side of the swimming pool, land him (with help if available) and commence resuscitation on dry land.

Training

In order to be proficient in the techniques of resuscitation, it is strongly recommended that all swimming teachers should undergo a course of instruction which includes practical experience using a resuscitation manikin. Full details of the skills described above, together with general and aquatic first aid, may be found in 'Resuscitation and First Aid' published by The Royal Life Saving Society U.K., Mountbatten House, Studley, Warwickshire, England B80 7NN (Telephone: Studley (052 785) 3943) from whom details of appropriate courses may also be obtained.

ASA
AWARDS SCHEME

The Amateur Swimming Association is the National Governing Body for the sport in England and has responsibilities ranging from Parent and Child water activities up to major competitions, from the training of teachers and coaches to healthy recreational swimming for all. Most people are unaware of the great range of work undertaken by the ASA.

The ASA Awards Scheme, sponsored by T.S.B. Bank, and offered in conjunction with the English Schools Swimming Association's Dolphin Trophy Scheme, for school children, sponsored by Coca Cola, is designed to reflect a good educational base with a logical progression from earliest stages to specialist disciplines.

You are urged to make full use of the scheme because of its educational base, and also because the revenue is ploughed back into the vast range of activities briefly noted in the first paragraph above.

The following is an outline of the scheme.

ASA/ESSA RAINBOW AWARDS SCHEME

There are 15 distance awards, recommended for children of 5 years and upwards, with tests of 5 metres to 5000 metres. There are no time limits. The new "Puffin" award is for swimming 5m with a buoyancy aid.

ASA/ESSA WATER SKILLS

There are 6 progressive grades testing skills such as swimming, floating, somersaulting, sculling, jumping and diving in, to name but a few.

NATIONAL CHALLENGE

There are 6 grades, the first two being ASA/ESSA, and the remainder ASA only. They test abilities on different strokes at different distances, sometimes with light clothing, combined with surface dives, to list but a few items.

PERSONAL SURVIVAL

The two levels test not only the physical ability of the performer, but also ask for knowledge of why given actions are made, and emphasise 'education for survival'.

ASA/ESSA SPEED SWIMMING

These awards are aimed at the average child and test speed in short dashes of 20 yards/metres, or 25 yards/metres on the 4 recognised strokes at Bronze, Silver and Gold standards. The Merit and Advanced Grades test a variety of strokes at longer distances, and with time limits.

The next three awards, Diving Skills, Water Polo Proficiency, and Synchronised Swimming are designed for the average child, and for instruction and testing by teachers with no special skills. The intention is to widen childrens' horizons and to give them a taste and choice of other disciplines.

PRELIMINARY DIVING SKILLS

The Star One and Star Two reflect the good teaching and safety required before attempting to dive. They lead to Novice Diver Three Star, which sets the performer on the right path to becoming a safe and skilled diver.

WATER POLO PROFICIENCY AWARDS

Available at Bronze, Silver and Gold Grades, these awards test individual and partner skills both static and moving. Any child who plays netball or football will enjoy them.

SYNCHRONISED SWIMMING

The Preliminary award will particularly attract and please girls with its gymnastic and artistic challenges. It leads to 5 more grades, each becoming more specialist in turn.

ULTIMATE SWIMMER

This award is aimed at developing and testing a wide range of skills in all disciplines. A log book is available in which a swimmer records awards successfully taken. When four named awards plus two chosen from four optional Awards have been completed the log book is sent to the ASA which recognises the level of achievement by giving a costume badge and a scroll free of charge.

SWIM FIT AWARDS

Aimed at the recreational swimmer, these awards recognise cumulative distances swum, regardless of style or speed. A green record card, completed on an 'honour basis' with no time limit, allows swimmers to complete 17 distances, from 10 to 1500 miles.

Further details and information on the Awards and Examiners from:–

The Awards Organiser,
Miss L. V. Cook,
12 Kings Avenue,
Woodford Green,
Essex IG8 0JB.

Telephone: 01-504 9361